The Complete Woodworking Course

The Complete Woodworking Course

Chris Simpson

B.T. Batsford · London

A QUARTO BOOK
First published in Great Britain by
B. T. Batsford Ltd.
4 Fitzhardinge Street, London
W1H 0AH

ISBN 0-7134-7648-6

A catalogue record for this book is
available from the British Library

This book was designed and produced by
Quarto Publishing plc
6 Blundell Street
London N7 9BH

Senior Editor Kate Kirby
Copy Editor Pamela Hopkinson
Senior Art Editor Mark Stevens
Designers Steve McCurdy, Tony Paine
Illustrators Rob Shone, Kuo Kang Chen
Plans David Kemp
Photographer Paul Forrester
Picture Manager Giulia Hetherington
Picture Researcher Susannah Jayes
Editorial Director Sophie Collins
Art Director Moira Clinch

Typeset in Great Britain by
West End Studios, Eastbourne
Manufactured by Eray Scan Pte Ltd,
Singapore
Printed by Star Standard Industries
(Pte) Ltd, Singapore

**With special thanks to Ian Styles of
Axminster Power Tools in Devon**

Contents

1 Foundation Course

2 Elementary Course

3 Intermediate Course

4 Advanced Course

How to Use This Book

Furniture making is mainly learned by doing it. All the teachers and books in the world can only provide information. Learning comes through doing. This book starts from the premise that anyone can learn the skills necessary to make beautiful and functional furniture. The book is in the form of a carefully structured course arranged in four parts, including a Foundation course, followed by Elementary, Intermediate and Advanced sections.

ABOUT THIS BOOK

This is not the kind of book you read through and then put down. It is a kind of workbook, full of specific instructions and advice. Try to think of it, as you read it, as your teacher speaking to you. This is a teacher you can turn to again and again.

Foundation course

If you have never done any woodwork before, then start here. The first part of the book introduces you to materials and tools. You learn about different timbers and their uses, and about the variety of manmade materials available today. Your first basic kit of hand tools is introduced, and you are shown how to use and care for your tools.

More experienced woodworkers will find this to be a valuable reference section as well.

Elementary course

This part of the course opens with background information on understanding working drawings and the principles of joining wood – basic information that will stand you in good stead through all your woodworking projects.

Technique sections introduce new skills that will be put to use in the modules. These are your practical lessons. Here you will learn, as if your teacher was standing beside you, how to perform the actions of measuring and marking, cutting, shaping, joining and finishing in clear, detailed step-by-step illustrations.

This is where you start to make your first pieces of furniture, a small table and a wall-hung cabinet. You will be guided every step of the way as you work through each module. Exploded diagrams and working drawings are supplied for each piece of furniture. The core of each module is a series of step-by-step photographs showing each stage in the woodworking process.

Intermediate course

The information is extended now, to bring

INFORMATION FEATURES

Practical information
Special information features introduce you to tools and materials. You will probably return to these time and again, dipping back into them to refresh your memory and increase your understanding as you progress through the course.

Theoretical information
These features outline the basic principles behind different aspects of woodworking. They clarify the reasons behind woodworking traditions, why certain joints work best in some situations and not in others, why furniture is made the way that it is.

Further Information
The cross-reference panel points you towards further information on the topic.

MODULES

Aims of the project
You will learn many things with each module, summarized here are the main techniques and skills.

Tools you will need
Tools listed in the order you will use them.

Time to allow
A rough estimate only, use this as a guide to help plan your work.

Remember
A reminder of some key points before you begin work.

Health and safety
So that you never forget you are working with potentially dangerous tools and equipment, you will be reminded of health and safety precautions before beginning each project.

Choosing wood
Suggestions for woods are provided to act as a guide when making your choice at your local timber yard.

Plans
Working drawings supply a detailed "pattern". Measurements of each component enable you to cross-refer to the cutting lists.

Scale
The scale enables you to relate the diagrams to the full size piece of furniture taking shape in your own workshop.

Exploded diagrams
The piece of furniture "taken apart" so you can clearly see how the joints are made and how every part relates to the whole.

Details
Selected details of the joints and construction techniques are further explained.

Further information
The cross-reference panel points you towards further information on the topic.

Step-by-step sequences
The author demonstrates each action for you, in colour photographs with clear and concise captions, almost as if you were working side by side.

Cutting list
The wood, and additional materials, that you will need to complete the piece of furniture. You must work from either metric or imperial measurements – they are not interchangeable.

Sawn measurements
The sawn measurements tell you what you need to buy from the timber yard.

Number of pieces
This tells you clearly the number of pieces to be cut in each size.

Planed measurements
You must reduce the wood to these measurements by planing before you begin the work of cutting and shaping.

No	Sawn	Planed
2	SIDES 610mm x 280mm x 25mm 2ft x 11in x 1in	560mm x 250mm x 20mm 1ft 10in x 10in x ¾in
1	TOP 432mm x 280mm x 25mm 1ft 5in x 11in x 1in	380mm x 250mm x 20mm 1ft 3in x 10in x ¾in
1	BOTTOM 432mm x 250mm x 25mm 1ft 5in x 10in x 1in	380mm x 235mm x 20mm 1ft 3in x 9¼in x ¾in
1	SHELF 380mm x 250mm x 20mm 1ft 3in x 10in x ¾in	356mm x 230mm x 12mm 1ft 2in x 9in x ½in
2	FOR FRAMED BACK STILES (UPRIGHTS) 610mm x 45mm x 25mm 2ft x 1¾in x 1in	565mm x 38mm x 20mm 1ft 10¼in x 1½in x ¾in
2	RAILS 406mm x 60mm x 25mm 1ft 4in x 2½in x 1in	356mm x 50mm x 22mm 1ft 2in x 2in x ⅞in
1	WALL BATTEN 305mm x 45mm x 12mm 12in x 1¾in x ½in	280mm x 35mm x 10mm 11in x 1⅜in x ¾in
1	BACK PANEL manmade board approx. 480mm x 305mm x 6mm 1ft 7in x 12in x ¼in	

+ masking tape, finishing, adhesive, 2 screws for cabinet back, wall fixings for batten in power tools and man-made materials and the different skills required to work with these. As you progress, you will continue to build on skills acquired earlier. Now you are introduced to more complicated constructions involving drawers, and to chair making.

The best of modern power and machine techniques are intro-duced alongside classic traditional hand skills.

Advanced course

You should be a skilled woodworker by now, ready to tackle complicated carcase constructions and hone your skills on fine woodworking projects. Advanced techniques of veneering, shaping, bending and laminating are introduced here, with the opportunity to put each into practice on the final modules – two fine boxes and an easy chair. If you have worked through all the modules in order, these should present no difficulty, you will be guided through in the same carefully thought out and detailed way.

TECHNIQUES FEATURES

Step-by-step sequences
Each new technique is introduced with a full demonstration, clear illustrations and captions. These are the actions you will practise over and over again and that will form the foundation of your woodworking skills.

Boxed features
Whenever extra detail or additional information is needed, you will find an occasional boxed feature. These aim to help you understand more about the technique you are learning, or perform it more efficiently and with greater understanding of the options available.

Further information
The cross-reference panel points you towards further information on the topic.

DESIGN FEATURES

Introduction
An introduction to the main features and developments in design of each piece of furniture covered in the modules.

Professional examples
Variations on each piece of furniture are to inspire you, and to demonstrate the different approaches of professional designers.

Design variations
Each piece of furniture can be varied in so many ways, and these illustrations aim to inspire you and widen your knowledge of design variations.

Principles of ergonomics
Illustrations show how the human body relates to furniture, these are the vital measurements and points on safety, comfort and ease of use that all furniture makers must consider.

Further information
The cross-reference panel points you towards further information on the topic.

SAFETY

Take sensible precautions and your workshop should be kept free from accidents. When dangers are recognized they can be avoided. Knowledge means good working practices, ignorance can lead to injury. Much safe practice is common sense and thinking ahead. It is also important to develop the correct attitude to tools – a balance of respect and caution.

Hand Tools
- Working practices have evolved so that cuts are made away from the body. Remember this and do not take risks.
- Keep tools sharp.

Power Tools
- Keep hands clear of moving blades and cutters.
- Read instructions thoroughly.
- Spend time looking at how the tool is made and works, with the power off.

Machinery
Realize what practices are potentially dangerous and avoid them by planning the job carefully.

- Always use push sticks.
- Always use the guards provided with the machinery.
- Remember that work can be caught by the saw or blade and thrown back at you.

Protection
- Whenever your eyes may be in danger, protect them by wearing safety spectacles, goggles or a mask.
- Wear ear protectors in noisy environments.
- Safeguard your lungs by wearing a mask or respirator.
- Use dust extraction on machinery.
- Ventilate effectively when finishing.
- Some adhesives and finishes can hurt the skin, so use gloves or barrier cream where necessary.

The Workshop
- Tidiness is important.
- Keep the space where you work clear of material.
- Do not smoke.
- Tidy dust and waste away regularly to prevent fire.
- Fit a smoke alarm.
- Keep a fire extinguisher in a prominent place.
- Keep a small first aid box for minor cuts and scratches.
- Include a pair of tweezers to remove splinters.

Goggles

Earmuffs

Dustmask

All-in-one respirator/visor

1 Foundation Course

All manner of people are drawn to the pleasures of woodwork, men and women, old and young, following many different trades and professions. What draws us all to this craft? Wood is good to use, it is clean, warm and natural, and our efforts result in pleasing and useful pieces. We use a material provided by nature which is ecologically sound. Wood lasts and wooden furniture often becomes an heirloom to hand on to future generations. Working with good tools is a pleasing and challenging part of the activity; and the mastery of skills gives a sense of achievement. This section introduces you to woods and materials and gives details of tools and how to use them – it covers the basic background information that you will need to know before starting. Enjoy learning and doing – and enjoy the results.

The Nature of Wood

Wood is a natural material, its very character and feel are a spur encouraging woodworkers to take up the craft. It is essential to have understanding of wood for effective and enjoyable working.

TREE GROWTH

The tree is a living organism that gives mankind great help – from oxygenating the planet to the provision of shelter and products. Water is drawn in through the roots and carbon dioxide taken in by the leaves, which then emit oxygen. Food is transmitted throughout the system.

Heartwood

Sapwood

Heartwood and sapwood
The wood near the centre of the trunk, the heartwood, carries little food, it is the structural support of the tree. The outer area transmits food and is called the sapwood. In some species only the heartwood is used for woodwork since the sapwood is weak and prone to fungal and insect attack, while in others there can be little difference, other than colour, between the two. ▲

Annual growth
The tree grows by adding to its girth each year, as well as to its height and spread. At the centre of the trunk is the pith or medulla – the remains of the sapling from which the tree grew. Then follows a series of annual rings, each depicting the growth cycle, normally of one year. Horizontal rays radiate from the centre. On the outside the cambium layer forms new wood, and bast and the bark ensure annual growth and protection. ◄

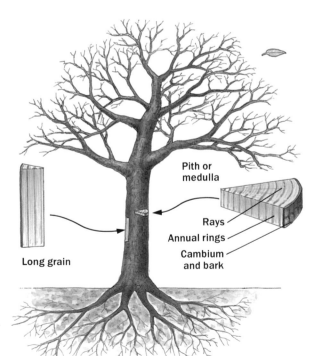

Long grain

Pith or medulla

Rays

Annual rings

Cambium and bark

SOFTWOODS AND HARDWOODS

These terms often cause confusion since they refer to the botanical characteristics of the tree. Some "hardwoods" are very soft – balsa wood for instance, while some "softwoods" can be quite hard – yew is botanically a softwood.

Softwoods
Softwoods come from coniferous trees with needles in place of leaves which tend to remain during winter. Softwoods are composed of tracheids, short cells where food and moisture are transmitted between the sides of adjacent cell walls. Softwoods may have vessels or pores, but these are generally channels for resin. ▼

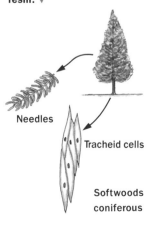

Needles

Tracheid cells

Softwoods coniferous

Hardwood vessels or pores

Broad leaf

Hardwoods deciduous

Ring porous

Diffuse porous

Hardwoods
Hardwoods come from deciduous trees, their leaves are shed in temperate climates each winter. The tree structure is made from long tubular vessels or pores which allow the tree to conduct moisture and food vertically. The horizontal rays carry food in a radial direction. Hardwood can be either ring porous or diffuse porous. Ring porous trees show clear annual rings marking the seasons, while diffuse porous trees live in areas where growth is year round. ▲

Quarter sawn

True quarter sawn

Through and through

Conversion

Timber is extracted from the forest as logs, mainly composing the trunk. Branch wood cannot usually be used since its structure has stresses and strains present. The log is converted into planks. Several different arrangements of cut are

used. The commonest is where the trunk is simply cut in a series of planks. However, the plank cut at the top tends to bow as it dries, and the annual rings try to straighten. Timber cut radially is very stable, therefore logs are often cut radially or quarter sawn. ▲

SEASONING

Converted timber still has moisture in the pores and cells, and this must be removed before the timber can be used. The wood is therefore dried or seasoned and the moisture content reduced to an acceptable level. For timber used in the open, moisture content of approximately 16 per cent is suitable. However, if it is to be used indoors, it must

be further reduced, down to 8 per cent, or even less in some cases.

Airdrying is the traditional method of seasoning. The cut log is placed in stick in the open, with some form of cover over it. As a general rule it takes one year for every 25mm (1in) thickness of the converted boards. This method will not reduce moisture to less than approximately 16 per cent

Re-stacking the planks
When the planks have been cut it is necessary to re-stack them in the order they were cut, with spacers between each plank to allow air to circulate. These spacers, called sticks, are always placed vertically above one another. ▲

and for interior work the boards have to be mechanically dried.

The modern method of drying is by putting the timber in kilns. The timber, in stick, is placed on trolleys and put into the kiln, a large oven in which the temperature and humidity are precisely controlled. The kiln cycle starts with high humidity which is carefully changed to ensure that the timber is dried at the correct rate. Timber can be damaged if the wrong kiln schedule is used.

A recently developed method, for small, valuable pieces of exotic timber, often used by wood turners is to soak the wood in PEG (Polyethelene Glycol) which chemically converts the moisture.

FAULTS IN TIMBER

Some timbers have a natural resistance to fungal and pest attack (i.e. teak) but others need treatment by preservatives to give the wood some resistance. Generally do not use wood in damp conditions where it may be attacked.

Faults may be found due to bad felling, poor seasoning, or erratic grain which causes trouble when timber is converted. Timber may have shakes, checking, splits, be in bow or in twist. When the board still has bark on it is called waney edged: it is advisable often with some timbers to remove the bark and sapwood since these attract pests – often in softwoods. Dead knots can be a problem as they will fall out and such timber should not be used in structural situations. In certain timbers live knots add to the unusual feature of the wood.

PROPERTIES OF WOOD

Grain in some woods is straight and even, but you will find cross grain which crosses in spirals around the tree, or interlocked grain when the spirals go different ways. Cross and interlocked grains are difficult to saw, plane and finish thus the saying "against the grain", but can result in attractive unusual features. Working "with the grain" is referred to frequently in the book.

Figure is when the grain runs in different directions, where the difference between early and late growth is marked, where colour is present, where there are unusual features such as curl or burr – these all contribute to interesting figure in wood. Texture can range from fine, when the cells are small, to an open or coarse texture when the cells are large.

FURTHER INFORMATION	
134-135	Veneers

TYPES OF WOOD

There are many different species of timber, and their distribution throughout the world means that you will find certain woods in your locality that will serve your purposes well. The following short selection of timbers is common in furnituremaking areas.

Common softwoods

Generally softwoods are used in building and joinery, but good quality softwoods should not be considered as being inferior to hardwoods. They have their own uses. The nomenclature is confusing, however, since their common names do not always indicate their true botanical classification.

SCOTS PINE (*Pinus* species) also known as European Redwood. Reasonable to work and has a very interesting figure. Its colour matures with age and it is one of the most attractive of the softwoods.

DOUGLAS FIR (*Pseudotsuga* species) Used for building.

SITKA SPRUCE (*Picea* species) Straight grain and even texture. Good to work, with a wide range of uses.

CEDAR OF LEBANON (*Cedrus* species) Good to work, but main attraction is its aroma, which is said to deter moths, so is often made into wardrobes.

YEW (*Taxus* species) Tough and hard. Difficult to work but the most beautiful of softwoods. Very good for fine furniture.

Common hardwoods

The following selection is arranged without any consideration of locality, since colour will direct choice.

OAK (*Quercus* species) Coarse textured and straight grained, with distinct rings in the quarter sawn.

ASH (*Fraxinus* species) Tough, straight grained and supple, a good wood for bending, with an attractive finish. Generally white, but with dark stained heartwood.

MAPLE (*Acer* species) Fine texture, hard and straight grained. Popular for furniture. Used for flooring.

BEECH (*Fagus* species) Straight grained, even textured, reasonable to work, good for steam bending. Often used in furniture, particularly chairs.

SYCAMORE (*Platanus* species USA, *Acer* species, Europe) Fine texture, generally straight grained (except for fiddleback grain used in musical instruments). Light in colour, good in taking stain.

CHERRY (*Prunus* species USA) Hard, fine textured and straight grained; attractive colouring, good for furniture.

MAHOGANY (*Swietenia* species) Medium texture, good to work, but many species and varies from light colour and weight, easy to work to species which are darker, heavier and hard.

WALNUT (*Juglans* species) Good to work, the better planks have lovely colour and grain. A lovely wood for all fine work.

TEAK (*Tectona* species) Substitutes – Iroko (*Chlorophora* species) and Afrormosia (*Pericopsis* species) Coarse texture but oily feel. Good to work but hard on edge tools requiring constant sharpening. Often used in the 1950s and 60s Scandinavian furniture with a simple oil finish.

ROSEWOOD (*Dalbergia* species)
Hard and heavy. Medium to work, but now very expensive and used for small fine work, inlay and veneer.

EBONY (*Diospyros* species)
Very hard and dense, difficult to work and one of the timbers nearest to the colour black.

PADAUK (*Pterocarpus*)
Hard, heavy and fair to work. When cut the shavings, sawdust and surface are bright red, but on exposure to light, the wood quickly goes dark brown.

Specialist woods
Some woods have become prized for specific uses.

BOXWOOD (*Buxus* species)
Fine textured, dense and heavy. Used for quality tool handles.

JELUTONG (*Dyera* species)
Soft and easy to work, a very good wood for pattern making, and carving.

LIGNUM VITAE (*Guaiacum* species)
Very hard and heavy. Close interlocked grain. Difficult to work. One of the heaviest and most resistant woods. Used for mallets and timber pulleys and bearings.

MANUFACTURED BOARDS

Manufactured boards have been made possible by developments in adhesive and resin technology. These boards are generally inert, so that timber movement is no longer a problem.

Plywood: Odd numbers of veneers are glued with the grain of each sheet at right angles to its neighbour. Plywood is normally available in sheets 1220mm x 2440mm (4ft x 8ft), often with a decorative face veneer on one or both sides which saves you having to veneer large surfaces. Plywood is made using different grades of adhesive — interior grade uses UF adhesives, while marine ply uses phenolic or Resourcinol-based adhesives.

3-Ply: Commonly used for drawer bottoms and cabinet backs; thicknesses can vary from 3mm (⅛in) to 6mm (¼in). Where the centre veneer is thicker than the face veneers, this is called stout heart.

Multiply: Available in a range of different thicknesses, used to construct furniture.

Birch ply: Use for superior performance and quality, especially when making preforms. It looks good on its own with the surfaces finished.

Blockboards: These are similar to plywood, except that the inner core is made of strips of wood. There are three grades, referring to the

width of the centre strips. Battenboard has the widest strips of all, in excess of 25mm (1in). Blockboard has strips of 6mm to 25mm (¼in to 1in). Laminboard generally has strips of 6mm (¼in) or less. The latter is the most stable, but also the most expensive.

Particle boards: Timber is reduced to fibres and then glued back into sheets with synthetic resins. Chipboard is used in the furniture industry and is available in several qualities.

Fibreboards: The edges of fibreboards need treating, generally by applying a solid or veneer lipping. Medium Density Fibreboard (MDF) has been developed for furniture, since its edge can be surfaced (by hand or machine) and it will take polish or finish directly.

FURTHER INFORMATION	
134-135	Veneers

Basic Hand Tools

The tools in this section provide a basic kit to start the projects in this book. Woodworking tools are precision instruments and their purchase, storage and use all need care if they are to last.

TOOL PURCHASE

Always buy the best tools you can afford, it is false economy to buy cheap ones. Price can be a guide but, more importantly, look closely at the tools and you will see the different qualities.

Buy tools made by a reputable manufacturer, but at this stage, do not be tempted to buy very expensive specialist handmade tools or antique tools since these are for the experienced woodworker.

Tool storage

Even a basic tool kit is a substantial investment, and to keep your tools in the best condition consider how you will store them.

The traditional woodworker's tool chest has a hinged top and a series of trays, with a large open well in the bottom.

Unless you have such a chest handed down, this is not the best type of modern tool storage since it is easy to lose tools at the bottom of the well.

The author's tool chest is like a cabinet with a door. The inside is fitted out with drawers, shallow ones at the top, deeper at the bottom. This way you can group tools according to their tasks.

There can also be problems with this design, since long tools will not fit unless you have a very large cabinet.

The very best way, if you have a secure, dry workshop, is to hang tools on wall-mounted boards. Each tool has its own place and is "shadowed" with a paint outline so you can see if one is missing.

Methods of storage
It is not always easy to keep tools to hand in a traditional woodworker's tool chest. ▲

A series of drawers means tools can be grouped according to task. ▲

Hang tools so that each has its own marked place. ▲

Workbench
A woodworking bench is one of the first things you will need.

The bench must be sturdily made, and heavy enough not to vibrate as you plane or saw. It is often useful to fit it to the floor or a wall.

The bench vice is an essential part of the bench. You will need one of the following types.

The integral vice has timber jaws tightened by rotating a screw. It is often supplied mounted on the front of the bench with another mounted on the end.

The metal vice is larger, and you need one of a good size, with minimum 230mm (9in) jaws with an opening width of up to 305mm (12in) preferably with a quick-release handle. You must fit hardwood vice "cheeks" to protect the work. ▲

1 Steel straight edge
Bevelled and about 1m (36in) long x 56mm (2¼in) wide x 5mm (³/₁₆in) thick, a straight edge is useful for marking with a knife and for checking straight edges.

2 Steel rules
These must have very clear markings for accuracy. A short one of 150mm (6in) another at 300mm (12in) and a longer one at 600mm (24in) are useful.

Retractable steel rules
These are popular and necessary for measuring anything over 1m (36in). They are unsuitable for fine work, but useful for marking timber before precise marking.

3 Try square
A try square is useful for marking right angles. Some are made for marking at 45 degrees, as well as at 90 degrees.

Steel combination square
With a cast metal stock which moves along the rule and locks in position, this is an alternative to a try square.

4 Pencil
A pencil is useful for initial marking out.

5 Marking knife
Use a marking knife for fine work and where you are marking prior to cutting or chiselling.

6 Marking gauge
The marking gauge has a stock sliding along a beam with a steel pin at one end which makes parallel marks. The stock is locked in place by a turn-screw.

Panel gauge
A panel gauge is similar to a marking gauge, with a longer beam and larger stock. It is used for marking wider boards.

7 Mortise gauge
A mortise gauge has two steel pins one of which is adjustable to set to the mortise chisel. The stock is also adjustable. It is used to mark mortises and tenons.

8 Metal bench dogs
These fit into holes drilled in the bench top to give a stop against which to work. Use them also with the end vice to hold or cramp.

9 G-cramps
In a range of sizes, these cramps are very useful to hold work or for assembly.

10 Sash cramps
Sash cramps are mainly an assembly tool, but they can be used for holding.

11 Ripsaws
Ripsaws are for ripping along the grain, crosscut saws for cutting across the grain. Ripsaw teeth are sharpened to act like chisels, while crosscut teeth are sharpened like small knives to sever the fibres.

Your initial purchase, however, should be a panel (or dual-purpose) saw that can be used for cutting both along and across the grain.

Backsaws
Backsaws have a strip of steel or brass along the back of the blade for stiffening. You will need two kinds.

12 Tenon saw
A tenon saw, from 305mm to 356mm (12in to 14in) long, is useful for all general purpose accurate crosscutting.

13 Dovetail saw
Typically 200mm to 250mm (8in to 10in) long, the dovetail saw is used for fine work as well as dovetails.

14 Coping saw
A coping saw is used for cutting curves. The fine-toothed blade is held in tension in a frame. The blade can be swivelled so that you can cut in any direction up to the depth of the throat.

Bench planes

Bench planes smooth wood, reducing it to required width or thickness, they true up boards, square off ends and smooth joints and surfaces before finishing. There are three main types.

15 Smoothing plane

This provides a smooth surface before finishing. However, since it is only up to 250mm (10in) long it often will not give a long flat surface.

Jack plane or fore plane

The jack plane or fore plane, between 355mm and 455mm (14in and 18in) long, is a good general purpose plane which can be used for rough smoothing, jointing or final smoothing.

16 Jointer or trying plane

This is 510mm to 610mm (20in to 24in) long. It is ideal for truing up boards, planing long edges straight and for general levelling.

You will need several different sizes of plane. Buy a jack plane first then,

a smoothing plane and finally a trying plane.

17 Hand scraper

This is a piece of tempered steel, generally measuring 100mm by 60mm (4in by 2½in) and 1.5mm (¹⁄₁₆in) thick. The two long edges are sharpened to produce a burr of metal which removes very fine shavings. Scrapers can also be curved for scraping curved surfaces.

18 Scraping plane

The scraping plane is a steel holder that ensures the

scraper blade is held in the right position and at the right angle.

19 Firmer chisels

Firmer chisels have blades that are rectangular in section for general work.

20 Bevel-edged chisels

These are less rigid since the sides of the blade are bevelled to give clearance for working in corners or where there are undercuts.

Start with a small selection of bevel-edged chisels in sizes 6mm, 12mm and 20mm (¼in,

½in and ¾in), then buy other sizes as you need them.

21 Mortise chisels

Mortise chisels are strong and heavy, to withstand hitting with a mallet. They are used for cutting out deep recesses or mortises. They range in size from 6mm to 12mm (¼in to ½in).

22 Mallet

The mallet is not only used for cutting mortises but is very useful for tapping joints together.

25 Countersink bits
Countersink bits for braces are also available. The auger bit is useful for drilling long and deep holes.

26 A wheelbrace with twist drills
This is better for fine work. Engineers' twist drills are useful in small sizes, but for 6mm (¼in) or larger holes, buy twist drills with centre points which are easier to use in wood.

27 Screwdrivers
These are necessary in a range of sizes, you will need at least three or four to start with.

28 Oilstone
An oilstone for keeping tools sharp is essential. When you are beginning, buy a stone with two faces — one with medium grit, the other with fine grit. Use light oil to lubricate the stone.

23 Pin hammer
A pin hammer for tapping in panel or veneer pins will be most useful for furniture projects in this book.

24 Brace and bits
For large work you will generally use the brace which takes a range of bits. Centre bits are the most common. You will need a range of sizes 6mm, 8mm, 10mm, 12mm and 20mm (¼in, ⁵⁄₁₆in, ⅜in, ½in and ¾in).

ABRASIVES

Use abrasives to prepare wood for finishing or to shape wood, particularly to round edges. Abrasives are graded by the coarseness of the grit: 600 is the finest and 50 is the coarsest. Abrasives may be used by hand or in power sanders. For a perfect finish work from coarse to fine grit, although planed or scraped surfaces may need only fine abrasives. For perfect finishes, rub down surfaces with fine abrasives between coats of wax, paint, lacquer or varnish.

TYPES OF ABRASIVE

Glass paper: This is used on softwoods and paintwork, it is not used for fine woodwork.

Garnet paper: Cuts cleanly leaving a smooth surface. It is available in very fine grit for hand or power sanding.

Aluminium oxide paper: Tends to be harder than garnet and often used with power tools. It lasts longer but does not give as fine a finish.

Silicon carbide paper: This is used by metalworkers as "wet and dry" paper, but furniture makers use a self-lubricating type, used dry, which is ideal for rubbing down a polished finish. Its hard grit makes it ideal for manmade boards which can be difficult to sand because of their high glue content.

Steel wool: In its fine grades is used for smoothing down between coats of finish or for applying wax.

grade	grit		applications
very coarse	50	1	heavy shaping
	60	1/2	
coarse	80	0	shaping – belt, disc, orbital and hand
	100	2/0	
medium	120	3/0	shaping and finishing – belt, disc, orbital and hand abrading
	150	4/0	
	180	5/0	
fine	220	6/0	finishing – power and hand abrading
	240	7/0	
	280	8/0	
very fine	320	9/0	final finishing, taking off sharp edges, sanding in between coats of lacquer hand abrading
	360		
	400		
	500		
	600		

Tool Maintenance

All woodworking tools need regular maintenance. Every tool with a cutting edge eventually becomes dull with use, and dull tools are unsafe as well as hard to use. New chisels and planes also need honing to a razor-sharp cutting edge before they are used for the first time.

Keep all tools clean, try to have a place in the workshop to store each one where it won't get knocked or damaged, and wipe over metal blades and parts with a light coating of oil to prevent rust.

Good tools are expensive and even a basic tool kit represents a substantial financial investment, yet sharp and properly maintained tools are a joy to use and will last a lifetime.

GRINDING AND SHARPENING

Plane blades, chisels and cutting gauges need to be ground and then sharpened on a stone.

● There are two main types of grinder, one of which is fluid lubricated. It is not advisable to use dry grinding wheels, as it is very easy to overheat the tool by over-zealous grinding, ruining the temper of the steel and the tool itself. If you have to use such a wheel, cool the tip of the tool *very* frequently in water. The use of fluid-cooled grinding machines, called slow speed motorized whetstones, is preferable. Some good small ones are available for the home workshop with either a horizontal stone disc or a vertical wheel, lubricated with water.

● Use a sharpening stone for sharpening and honing. There are several different types, but when starting out you will probably use a synthetic stone made from aluminium oxide or silicon carbide and lubricate it with light machine oil. You will need several grades of oilstone, and it is possible to buy a combination stone. Choose one with medium and fine grades. As you progress with woodworking you may like to consider some of the alternatives to synthetic stones. Natural Arkansas stones are excellent oilstones. Japanese water stones have a wide range of hardness grades, while diamond sharpening stones are also available.

● Where the lubricating medium is oil, it is necessary to keep the surface clean. After much use, the stone will become clogged and need cleaning with paraffin. A waterstone needs to be immersed in water to saturate it and it must be kept wet during use.

● For final honing after using an oil stone, use a leather strop with stropping paste, fine carborundum powder or jeweller's rouge to produce a razor-sharp edge.

● If your stone becomes hollow after repeated sharpening, it can be flattened by grinding on a sheet of plate glass with carborundum powder as a cutting agent. (See note on surfacing the sole of planes, this is basically the same technique.)

MAINTAINING AND ADJUSTING PLANES

A modern metal plane is a precision tool and requires precise adjustment every time the blade is removed for sharpening. Even once it is set up, the blade can be knocked out of true by a jolt or by dropping on the bench.

Protect the plane blade by retracting it each time you store the plane. Store it on its side on a shelf, or in its box. Wipe it over with an oily cloth occasionally to prevent rust.

If you have difficulty planing smoothly, check the metal casting to see that the sole is perfectly flat. On a quality tool this should be the case, but if it is not, you can flatten the bottom of the plane by applying some carborundum powder to a sheet of glass and rubbing the plane over it. This is a lengthy process, but should result in a finely tuned tool.

SHARPENING PLANES

Some woods blunt plane blades very quickly and with difficult timbers you may need to sharpen a plane blade every ten minutes or so; but even with the best timber, you will still need to stop and sharpen the blade more often than you might at first expect.

Plane blades are normally sharpened at two angles. The ground angle of 25 degrees, which you should not need to touch for some time, and the sharpening angle of 30 degrees which you will probably have to hone before you start work and which requires regular sharpening.

A plane blade needs a razor-sharp edge, and to get the sharpest blade possible, use an oilstone followed by a leather strop with some very fine carborundum powder or jeweller's rouge. You should be able to see and feel the sharpness of the blade at this stage. However, in feeling the edge, be careful not to cut yourself.

When you first buy a new plane, it is worth taking it carefully apart so that you are familiar with its components and how they work. It is useful to tune or humanize a new tool by giving some attention to smoothing the handles and removing any sharp edges on top of the plane that might make its use uncomfortable.

Anatomy of a plane

1 Lever cap
2 Locking lever
3 Cap iron
4 Blade
5 Cap iron locking screw
6 Frog
7 Lever cap screw
8 Lateral adjustment lever
9 Depth adjustment lever
10 Depth adjustment wheel
11 Sole
12 Rear handle
13 Front knob
14 Mouth

Dismantling and sharpening a plane blade

1 To remove the blade, lift the lever, this releases pressure on the blade and allows removal of the lever cap. ▶

2 Lift the blade and cap iron out of its seating and, holding the blade and cap iron assembly, loosen the screw holding the two together, and remove the cap iron. ▶

3 To sharpen the blade, rub the angled side on an oilstone. The other side must be left perfectly flat. Hold the blade firmly, keeping the angle, about 30 degrees. Work the blade backwards and forwards along the oilstone. ▶

FURTHER INFORMATION

| 9 | Safety first |

4 A burr or sliver of metal will now have appeared on the other (flat side) of the blade. Carefully remove this by laying this face of the blade flat on the oilstone, and taking a few strokes. Repeat the process of honing and removing the burr. For a razor-sharp final edge, use a leather strop. ▲

Replacing the blade and adjusting the plane

1 Fit the cap iron back onto the blade. To avoid spoiling the sharp edge, rotate the cap iron in position behind the front edge and carefully move it forward to within about 1mm (1/32in) of the edge. The nearer the cap iron is set to the blade, the finer the cut. ▼

2 Make sure the cap iron and blade fit tightly together to prevent shavings wedging between them. Carefully set the blade and cap iron back into the plane and lock in place using the lever cap. ▶

3 Hold the plane at eye level and sight along the sole to see the projecting blade. Use the lateral adjustment lever to make sure the blade projects parallel with the sole across its width. Move the lever from side to side. ▶

4 Depth of cut increases as the blade is pushed out by turning the depth adjustment nut. The cutting edge should appear as a fine black line. For fine work the blade should hardly be visible. ▶

MAINTAINING AND SHARPENING CHISELS

Like a plane blade, a chisel has a ground angle and a sharpening angle. The manufacturer supplies the chisel already ground to an angle of 25 degrees; you will not generally have to work on this angle, but the cutting edge of the chisel must be honed to between 30 degrees and 35 degrees and kept razor sharp by regular honing on an oilstone.

Protect chisels when not in use by storing them carefully, either in a wall-mounted rack, if you have the space, or by keeping them rolled up in a cloth.

Sharpening a chisel blade

1 Hold the blade at the correct angle and move it with a forwards and backwards motion along the oilstone. Put pressure on as you move forwards, release it as you move backwards. ▲

2 Be sure to keep the edge that is being produced square with the edge of the chisel blade. After a few strokes, check to see that the bevel is forming evenly and test with your thumb to feel if the burr is forming on the back. ▲

3 Remove the burr by stroking the back of the chisel flat on the sharpening stone. Repeat the process of honing and de-burring as for the plane blade, and finish off on a leather strop. ▼

4 When sharpening narrow blades it is important that you do not wear a groove in the oilstone. Move blades about in a figure-of-eight to utilize the whole surface of the stone, being careful not to dig the edges of the blade into the stone. Very narrow blades may be sharpened on the edge of the stone. ▼

MAINTAINING SAWS

A sharp saw needs no forcing through the wood, but a blunt saw cuts slowly and will wander from the cutting line, and may jam or buckle if forced. The saw is one tool which is difficult for an amateur to sharpen. Good "saw doctors" as they are known, need a lot of time and experience to perfect their skills, and many woodworkers prefer to send their saws to a saw doctor rather than do it themselves.

Many modern saws are available with hard-tipped blades which last much longer than traditional blades, but which cannot be re-sharpened.

Coping saw blades are disposable and should be replaced as soon as they become blunt.

Whether you use traditional or modern hard-tipped blades, you can prolong the life of all your saw blades by keeping them clean, wiping the blades over with an oily cloth occasionally and protecting them from damage when not in use.

The teeth can be protected by slotting a piece of plastic clip or purpose-made plastic extrusion over them, and if possible, hang each saw up on the workshop wall.

Hanging saws

1 The best way of hanging saws is to make a shaped block that fits into the hand-hold in the saw handle, with a rotating toggle to hold the saw in place. ▲

2 Handsaws can be supported at their blade end with a timber "bridge" over the blade, while backsaws can have their tooth resting in a groove in a piece of wood. This also protects the blade. ▲

FURTHER INFORMATION	
9	Safety first
24-25	Planing
26	Chiselling
26-27	Sawing

Planing

Planing prepares the wood for accurate marking and cutting out of joints, and smooths the wood ready for finishing processes. The plane blade must be razor sharp and carefully adjusted to take shavings of the depth required. Planing is a skill that takes practice to acquire – be prepared to spend quite a lot of time getting used to the tool, and to learning the techniques needed to sharpen, adjust and use it accurately.

Planing sequence

There is a sequence to planing that should be followed at nearly all times. Plane the face side, then the face edge. Then gauge and plane to width, and finally plane to thickness. Sawing a component exactly to length is left until later.

Choice of plane

A long plane gives a more accurate result, it rides over the high spots on the wood, gradually removing them until the wood is even and a single long shaving can be taken off. A smaller plane follows the contours of the surface. A smoothing plane or small jack plane makes a good choice for a first buy.

Set the plane to take a fine cut at first until you are used to the action. There is less resistance and more control than if you set the blade to take a thicker cut. As you plane, adjust the blade until you are taking a good shaving from the surface.

HOW TO PLANE

1 Begin by choosing the better side of the board, this will become the face side. Hold the board on a firm horizontal surface, against a bench stop, or in a vice for small pieces. Stand with shoulder, hip and plane in line for full control, feet slightly apart. ▼ ▶

2 Aim to work with a smooth motion, applying even pressure. As you pass the plane over the wood at the beginning of the stroke, pressure is on the front handle. ▶

3 In mid-stroke, press evenly, and as you reach the end of the stroke, transfer pressure to the rear handle. Don't lift the plane up until the plane blade is beyond the end of the board. ▶

Squaring the wood: Planing face side, face edge, width and thickness
Think of planing and checking for straightness and squareness as one skill, one is of little use without the other. Stop frequently to check the wood. Always lay the plane on its side when you put it down, to prevent the blade being damaged.

4 As you plane the face, stop and check the wood carefully for flatness across the width; and sight along the wood to check it for straightness. ▲

5 To check for "winding" or twisting, place two wooden battens at each end and sight across the tops to see if they are parallel. ▲

6 Place a steel rule or straight edge along the grain at intervals to check the surface is flat along its whole length. Alternatively tilt the plane on its side and use that as a straight edge. ▲

Planing the edge

7 To plane the face edge, put the timber against a bench stop or in a vice. To keep the plane centred on a narrow edge, put the thumb on top of the sole near the handle and run the fingers along under the side to guide the plane. ▼

8 Use a square to check that the edge is square with the face along its whole length. Be sure to push the stock of the square tight up against the face side of the wood. Hold the wood up to the light if possible. ▼

Marking and planing the other sides

9 Once you have a face and edge that are perfectly straight and at right angles to one another, mark them with the face and edge mark. With these surfaces true, it is relatively easy to make the timber the width and thickness you need for your project. ▶

10 Use a marking gauge to mark the width of the board from the face edge. Set the gauge to the width, hold the stock against the face edge, and gauge a line.
Turn the board over to mark the width on the sawn, unplaned side. Again, run the stock of the gauge against the face edge. Plane, or saw and plane, the board to this width, checking frequently. ▶

11 To mark the thickness required, run the stock of the marking gauge against the face side, marking a line on the face edge and one on the far edge. Then plane the board down to these marks. Stop and check the work often for squareness. ▶

Planing wide boards

Plane wide boards, or boards that have been joined together, working diagonally, with and across the grain in overlapping strokes to cover the whole surface. Finish by taking fine shavings in parallel strokes in the direction of the grain. ▼

FURTHER INFORMATION	
9	Safety first
16-19	Basic hand tools
20-23	Tool maintenance
130-131	Power planing

Chiselling

Sawing

The action of chiselling is called paring. Depending on the task, you will either be paring vertically, or paring horizontally. Sometimes you will be working to cut away a complete end or face; at other times, particularly to make joints or to cut housings, say for hinges, you only need to chisel part-way through the wood.

Always work to a marked line and work within the waste area first, carefully paring wood away up to the marked line. Remove only small amounts of wood at a time. As a general rule, cut the wood across the grain first, make any cuts along the grain afterwards, to avoid splitting the wood.

A narrower chisel gives you more control as it has less resistance from the wood.

Secure the wood firmly, and if you are going to cut right through it, place a piece of scrap wood beneath it to protect the workbench.

Holding the chisel

Always hold the chisel in such a way that you cannot cut yourself, keeping hands behind the cutting edge at all times. Use one hand to guide the chisel blade, while the other hand holds the chisel and supplies the force required.

PARING VERTICALLY

Hold the chisel bevel outwards. One hand guides the blade to remove small amounts of wood each time, working up to the cutting line. With the other hand apply the pressure, from the shoulders.

When working across the grain, sever the fibres with a series of parallel cuts to loosen them before making the final cut to the line. ▲

PARING HORIZONTALLY

1 Hold the chisel bevel upwards. The thumb on the blade acts to guide the chisel, while the other hand applies the pressure. ▶

2 For additional power, lean into the work, applying body pressure from the waist. ▶

USING A MALLET

Chisels are only hit with mallets, never hammers. Normally a chisel should be sharp enough to do its work without being hit by a mallet, although most modern chisels are tough enough to withstand tapping with the mallet. Generally you only hit a mortise chisel, or a firmer chisel when removing waste from housings. ▶

Accurate sawing takes a lot of practice, but it calls for precision on your part, not force. The aim is to let the saw do the work, a good saw should feel well-balanced and cut smoothly almost under its own weight. Your task is to guide the saw, not to press it down.

The steps shown here refer to cutting across the grain, and cutting right through a piece of wood. When you are cutting joints you will be using the same technique to cut along the grain or only part-way through the wood.

3 After the first few strokes you should have the beginnings of a saw cut. Now start taking longer, steady strokes. Watch the pencil line across the face side and direct the cutting edge of the saw to the waste side of that line. ▼

SAWING PRACTICE

1 Holding a square against the face side and face edge, mark pencil lines across the timber on the face side and down the face edge. ▲

2 Hold the wood firmly and stand so that the blade is in line with your arm and shoulder. Start the cut with a few strokes on the far corner, guiding the blade against your raised thumb. ▲

4 Saw steadily, and keep checking that your cut is remaining on the line, both across the face and then as it starts to go down the edge. ▼

PRECISION SAWING

1 Now you are used to the action, practice more precise sawing. Using a knife mark a cut line on all four surfaces. Start the saw cut on the face side at the far edge, as in step 2 left. ▶

2 Saw on the waste side of the marked line, watching continually that you do not wander from it. Saw carefully with the saw at a high angle, then lower the saw to begin cutting across the face side. ▶

3 Once you have made a kerf on the face side for the saw to run in, start cutting down the face edge. You will see that you have now cut a triangle as defined by these two faces. ▶

4 Sawing the third surface is relatively easy because the cuts already made will guide the saw and you should be able to concentrate on watching the line and checking that the blade is not deviating from the cut that you have made. ▶

5 As you complete the cut, go carefully with the final few strokes. Support the end of the wood with your hand so that the offcut does not fall and splinter the board. ▲

FURTHER INFORMATION	
9	Safety first
16-19	Basic hand tools
20-23	Tool maintenance

It is exciting to see a piece of furniture take shape. In this chapter, the first two modules introduce basic frame and carcase structures. The small table is an ideal project to introduce mortise and tenon joints, and the cabinet gives you your first experience of making dovetails. Both projects are fairly simple but will give you the chance to master preparation, marking, jointing, assembly and finishing. This experience, once mastered, provides the basis for the other projects. At this stage take it steady. Do not worry about mistakes and gain the basic skills that will bring much reward later.

Reading Drawings

All but the simplest projects require an accurate scale drawing to be completed before making any piece of furniture. The drawing allows you to check proportions, measurements and construction details. There are basic drawing conventions followed by designers of all kinds, including furniture designers. These conventions, once you understand them, speed up the drawing process and remove any possibility of misunderstanding between designer and maker.

As an example, Module 2, the wall-hung cabinet, is used here to demonstrate various drawing techniques and conventions.

SKETCH DRAWINGS AND 3D PROJECTIONS

Nearly all designers will begin with rough sketches, working them up to progressively more detailed and accurate drawings. Even if you have no drawing skills, you can still follow the same process using the drawing conventions and the basic projections.

Projections allow a 3-dimensional object to be represented on a flat piece of paper. This exploded 3D view of the wall-hung cabinet is a sophisticated illustration of an isometric projection, but it still keeps to certain basic conventions which any one can follow with the help of a T-square and a 30/60 degree try square. All vertical lines are drawn vertically and all other lines are drawn at 30 degrees to the horizontal.

Exploded diagrams
Exploding the components enables hidden details to be clearly seen. The exploded drawing can be used to begin to work out proportions.

Details of joint construction can be accurately worked out.

For accurate working, this joint detail will need to be drawn up as a full size plan later.

SCALE DRAWINGS

Most drawings need to be reproduced to scale if they are to be a manageable size. The scale chosen should suit the size of the object being drawn and will always be indicated on the drawing.

Again, there are conventions in the choice of scale which most designers will follow. For individual pieces of furniture a scale of 1:5 in metric measurements is common. This means 1cm or 10mm on the drawing equals 5cm or 50mm on the piece of furniture. In imperial measurements the convention is to use a scale of 1:4 meaning ¼in = 1in or 3in = 1ft.

For larger pieces of furniture or room layouts, scales of 1:20 metric and 1:24 imperial are common.

Small items or details may be drawn fullsize or even larger, and joints, mouldings and other details are often drawn alongside scale drawings of the whole piece of furniture. It is quite common for drawings to include several items at different scales.

In recording dimensions, the convention is to write

Types of projection
A first angle projection imagines the object suspended in a square corner and being projected back onto the three surfaces ▼

In a first angle projection, the corner is cut, along the red line, and opened out flat to produce the drawing. ▼

all measurements between extension lines for clarity. All dimensions should be placed so that they are readable from the bottom righthand corner of the drawing.

Dimensions should be complete enough for full cutting lists to be worked out from them.

The first angle

A third angle projection imagines each face of the object projected forwards onto a glass corner. ▼

The glass corner is cut and opened out flat to produce the drawing. ▼

projection and the third angle projection are commonly used for accurate scale drawings. Both make use of the front view (front elevation), placing side views to left or right, and a plan view to top or bottom.

Third angle projection

The third angle projection is one method of laying out a drawing. ▶

"Grain" lines are an accepted convention to represent sections through solid timber.

B-B, indicated here, relates to the further internal details that are included on the plan view.

A detail clarifies the way in which the back components fit together and the way the cabinet attaches to the wall batten. ▶

Broken lines indicate where the full size drawing has been "compressed" to exclude parts that do not require this detailed treatment.

Here, the plan view includes a sectional half plan taken through B-B (below).

The front elevation enables accurate internal and external dimensions to be shown.

Sectional views are slices through the work to show internal construction details. This sectional side elevation has been taken through the centre line or A-A.

Other types of plan

You will encounter other types of drawings in books and woodworking magazines.

A popular convention is to use a scaled-down grid over a drawing, such as the one used in Module 8, the easy chair. This is particularly useful when components require curves and shaping. Draw up a fullsize grid and plot where the lines of the drawing intersect with the grid.

A 3-dimensional cut-away drawing with detail annotations is another way of showing how intricate or shaped components fit together. ▲

FURTHER INFORMATION	
62-67	Module 2: wall-hung cabinet

Basic Jointing

Generally woodworkers have to deal with material in the form of boards. Because timber has a grain direction joints have evolved to suit different configurations.

JOINTING AND GLUING

With glue technology as advanced as it is, why have joints at all? Joints have evolved so that their mechanical strength is as important as the addition of any adhesive.

End grain cannot be glued effectively, any attempt to join end-to-end or end-to-edge results in a poor bond. A face-to-face adhesive bond is reasonably strong. Joining long edge to long edge gives a very good bond as does joining an edge to a face.

Good jointing aims for mechanical strength and the best gluing situation where as much wood as possible is jointed face to face. A simple bridle joint for example has poor gluing between shoulders and the face but good gluing between the face and the joint.

JOINT DEVELOPMENT

Most joints have evolved as a variation on a peg fitting into a hole to make a mechanical connection.

Principles of joints

Boards meeting edge-to-edge call for two possible approaches: a simple glued butt joint, or the addition of mechanical means, with tongue and groove, loose tongue, dowels or biscuits. ▼

A flat timber frame can use mitres, halving joints, bridle joints, dowels or mortise and tenons. In manmade board you would try to cut from the whole board. ▼

A rail and stile or underframe arrangement would use mortise and tenons. These may be through, and may be wedged, or stopped. Jointing this arrangement in manmade board is not appropriate. ▲

For a corner joint use a dovetail. Or use a simple butt or mitre joint reinforced with veneer keys, dowels, loose tongues or biscuits. ▲

To fit a partition use either a stopped or a dovetail housing. Manmade boards could use a housing but a tongue, biscuit, or butt joint may be sufficient. ▼

TYPES OF JOINTS

Edge-to-edge butt joint

Traditionally a rubbed joint. With modern glues and cramps can be simply glued together. Not very strong. Use for table tops; panels. ▲

Butt joint

Mechanically strengthened with tongue and groove, loose tongue in two grooves, dowels or biscuits. The board faces come precisely together, reducing planing. Use for table tops; wide panels. ▲

Mitre joint

Needs reinforcing with a veneer pin, dowels or tongues. Decorative keys or splines cut from wood or veneer can be glued in. Use for picture frames; framing a central panel. ▲

Halving joint

One of the simplest joints for two pieces meeting in an L or T or cross formation. May be pegged through with dowels. Not very strong. Use for small simple frames; cabinet door frames. ▼

Bridle joint

An open mortise and tenon — the tenon is usually one-third the thickness of the wood, unless connecting pieces of different thicknesses. Use for leg and rail connection on tables. ▼

Dowel joint

Widely used as a substitute for mortise and tenons. Strong and easy to make. Use for cabinet frames; doors; table tops; table frames. ▼

Through mortise and tenon
The tenon goes through the mortise and is often wedged. The strongest end to edge joints. Use for frames in cabinetmaking; table underframes; chair frames; door frames. ▲

Stopped mortise and tenon with shoulders
Used in good quality furniture making. A strong rigid joint. Use for cabinet frames; chair frames. ▲

Sloping haunch
Used when the mortise is near the top of a leg or rail. Use for cabinet frames; table frames. ▲

Double mortise and tenon
Where a wide rail goes into a vertical stile. Use for table frames; chair frames; door frames. ▶

Through dovetail
Strong and attractive. The finger or comb joint is machine-made. Use for boxes; drawers. ▶

Single lap dovetail
The end grain is hidden on one piece. Use for joining drawer sides to drawer fronts. ▶

Double lap dovetail
The dovetail is hidden. Only the thin line of end grain on the tail part is visible. Use for cabinets. ▶

Secret mitre dovetail
A difficult joint to make. From the outside looks like a simple butted mitre. Use for cabinet construction; drawers. ▶

Reinforced butt joint
Using screws or pins, or mitre joints reinforced with dowels. Use for cabinet corners; picture frames. ▶

TYPES OF ADHESIVE

Polyvinyl-acetate (PVA)
A very good general purpose adhesive convenient and readymixed in the form of a creamy liquid.
- For internal use
- Limited external use
- Long or short drying times available
- Wood or manmade board

Urea formaldehyde (UF)
Before the latest developments of PVA, UF was always reckoned the best glue for woodworking. It is available most commonly as a powder which you mix with water (one-shot). A twin-pack of resin and hardener is preferable since with one-shot the ratio of powder to water needs careful control. The glue should be like thick cream, well stirred to prevent lumps.
- The best for pre-forming
- For internal and external use
- Wood or manmade board

Natural glues
Traditional animal glue is still used for hand-veneering. Casein, a by-product of milk, is unusual these days but if renovating old furniture you may well use an animal glue.
- Furniture restoration
- Veneering

Stopped housing joint
An effective and easy joint. Stopping the housing gives an unbroken vertical line on the carcase. Use for fixing shelves; holding rails inside carcases. ▶

Bare-faced tapered dovetail housing
Should need no cramping. A strong joint. Use for fixing shelves. ▼

Small Table

The techniques and processes used in making this small table can be applied to many other designs which use a frame construction. The finished table is a classic, timeless design. Its construction covers many of the processes that will form the basis of further projects: timber selection and conversion, measuring and marking, cutting joints, making a mitred frame, and finishing.

In later projects and as your tool kit increases, you may consider using power hand tools or machinery. However, at this stage "bite the bullet" and master these basic processes by hand. The feel of the hand tool is basic to an understanding of the material.

AIMS OF THE PROJECT
Provide a foundation in basic techniques and processes. Precision cutting and fitting of a number of identical joints.

TOOLS YOU WILL NEED
Chalk
Pencil
Rule
Try square
Panel saw
Marking gauge
Marking knife
Jack plane
Tenon or dovetail saw
Mortise chisel
Bevel edge chisels
Mortise gauge
Rebate plane or shoulder plane
Drill and drill bits
Nail punch
4 Sash cramps
Cabinet scraper
Sanding block

TIME TO ALLOW
If this is your first project, much time will be spent in learning basic processes and developing skills, so be prepared to spend what time is necessary to achieve the best possible result.

REMEMBER
Read through the instructions and plan the project in your mind.

HEALTH AND SAFETY
Follow the safe working procedures outlined on page 9.

CHOOSING WOOD
Your choice will be based on colour, workability, availability and cost. Hardwood is preferable to softwood when beginning furnituremaking. Joinery softwoods are not recommended, since they do not saw or chisel crisply. For this first project buy timber with a straight grain. You will not need to maximize grain pattern or avoid defects, so marking out will be simplified.

Colour Choose a timber that will relate to the place where the table will be used. Lighter woods could be English oak, American white oak or beech, maple or sycamore. Medium woods could be mahogany, teak or American red oak and dark woods could be American black walnut, French walnut, or rosewood.

Workability Choose a wood that works well, is not so soft that it is difficult to achieve crisp saw and chisel cuts, nor so hard that it is brittle. The wood should have a close grain and good working properties.

CUTTING LIST

No	Sawn	Planed
4	LEGS 560mm x 40mm x 40mm 1ft 10in x 1½in x 1½in	480mm x 30mm x 30mm 1ft 7in x 1¼in x 1¼in
4	TOP RAILS 305mm x 50mm x 25mm 12in x 2in x 1in	240mm x 45mm x 20mm 9½in x 1¾in x ¾in
4	BOTTOM RAILS 305mm x 40mm x 25mm 12in x 1½in x 1in	240mm x 30mm x 20mm 9½in x 1¼in x ¾in
4	TOP FRAME SIDES 406mm x 80mm x 25mm 1ft 4in x 3¼in x 1in	350mm x 75mm x 20mm 1ft 2in x 3in x ¾in

+ masking tape, finishing, adhesive, dowels, screws and sheet material for inset top measuring 230mm x 230mm x 6mm (9in x 9in x ¼in)

PLANS

The drawings on this page show the elevations and sections, together with an exploded perspective view of the finished piece.

Scale 1:11

350mm 1'2"
12mm 1/2"
260mm 10½"
200mm 8"

Plan · 20mm 3/4"
Plan with top removed

45mm 1 3/4"
500mm 1'7¼"
30mm 1¼"
430mm 1'7"
150mm 6"

Front elevation

Tenons are mitred at meeting faces

Exploded diagram

Side elevation

Sectional end elevation

FURTHER INFORMATION	
30-31	Reading drawings
56-57	Principles of frame construction

TIMBER PURCHASE

1 Buy wood in the sawn plank. You must make an allowance for waste in converting it from its sawn state to planed to size.

The length of 240mm (9½in) for the rails allows 200mm (8in) between shoulders plus 20mm (¾in) each end for tenons. Two thicknesses of board are needed 40mm and 25mm (1½in and 1in). Buy one plank of each thickness from which to cut the components.

MARK AND CUT COMPONENTS

2 Mark the components on to the sawn board with chalk, making an allowance for the saw cuts. ▼

3 Cut the components from the marked board, using a panel saw.

4 Plane all components and mark them with face and edge marks.

MARK OUT LEGS OF TABLE UNDERFRAME

5 Mark the four legs together. Set the legs with the face sides uppermost and the face edges towards you. Hold them together with a cramp. ▲

6 Using a pencil, mark the length of the legs and the position where the rails will be fitted. Then mark the length of the mortises.

The lower rails have a small 3mm (⅛in) shoulder on the top and the bottom. The top rails have a shoulder on the bottom and a sloping haunch at the top. A haunch is a shortened portion of the tenon, it helps lock the joint to prevent the frame twisting out of line.

7 Hatch in the mortise waste. Then at the top and bottom of the legs at the mortise positions, mark a cut line with a marking knife 3mm (⅛in) inside the pencil marks indicating the rail positions at the ends of the mortises.

TRANSFER MARKS TO THE FACE EDGE

8 Uncramp the four legs and, with a try square, transfer all the pencil marks from the face side to the face edge. Then transfer the cut lines on the ends and at the ends of the mortises, and pencil in the waste. This will give you four legs, with joints marked on the eight inside faces. Complete the top and bottom cut lines all round the legs.

GAUGE MORTISES

9 Set the mortise gauge pins to the width of the mortise chisel at the pin points. Then set the gauge so that the mortise marks are central on the legs; do this by marking the points from one side, then turning and marking from the other side, adjusting to correct any discrepancy. Make the marks from the face side and edge.

10 Mark out the eight rails of the table underframe, four top and four bottom. Cramp the upper set together, and mark the lengths on the four face edges with a marking knife. Mark the length of 200mm (8in) between the shoulders, plus an extra 20mm (¾in) on each end for the tenons, giving a total length of 240mm (9½in). Take off the cramp. ▼

11 Now repeat this procedure with the lower set of rails cramped together. Use the cut lines on one of the top rails to mark the precise position on this set, to ensure both are exactly the same.

12 Check the marking and transfer these lines to the other three faces of each rail. Always use the square from the face side or the face edge. ▲

13 Cut the rails exactly to length. Then, with the pins of the mortise gauge as already set to the mortise chisel, adjust the stock to centre on the rails and mark the tenons round the end of the rails. Now mark the shoulders and haunches on the tenon sides, using a marking gauge. Pencil the waste that will be removed. Re-check all marking.

CUT MORTISES IN LEGS

14 There are 16 mortises to cut in the legs. Remember to cut to the shoulder line, not the pencilled position of the rail. ▲

15 Hold the work in the vice and chop out the waste up to the lines.

16 In the eight mortises for the top rails, make the entry for the haunch, saw down at the ends of the mortise. ▼

17 Chop out the waste to accept the haunch. ▼

SAW TENONS ON RAILS

18 There are eight tenons with haunch and shoulder, and eight with two shoulders. Saw down to the shoulders on all tenon pieces in the same way. Then cut the sloping line of the haunch. ▶

FURTHER INFORMATION	
26	Chiselling
26-27	Sawing
44-46	Making a mortise and tenon joint

19 Lay each piece flat to cut the main tenon shoulder. ▼

DRILLING FOR THE POCKET SCREWS

20 Mark two drill holes in the underside of each top rail for the pocket screws to hold the top frame. With a small table like this it would be difficult to drill the top rails to accept pocket screws after the frame is glued up.

21 Counterbored screws are needed when a deep rail is to have a top attached by screws. To simply drill a clearance hole for the screw, with the screw head at the bottom face of the rail, would require very long screws. Therefore, drill a hole larger than the screw head only part way through the rail, from the underside. The screw then sits in a hole at a pre-determined depth, allowing a shorter screw to be used.

Mark carefully, drill the clearance hole for the screw, then counterbore for the screw head to the required depth. ▼

NUMBER AND FIT ALL JOINTS

22 Number or letter each joint and carefully fit each tenon into its mortise. With practice it will be possible to make the mortise and tenon so they fit accurately from the saw, but it is likely that for some time you will have to pare with a chisel to fit the joints. ▲

23 It is standard practice, as in this design, for the rails on all four sides to be at the same level. Therefore the tenons at each corner will meet and it is necessary to cut a mitre on the end of each tenon so they fit in the mortise together. Check and re-check that you have marked this correctly before you cut.

FINISH INTERNAL FACES

24 You will soon be ready to prepare for assembly, but with this design it is best to finish all the internal faces first. Scrape and sand the four faces of each rail and the two inside faces of each leg. Then mask all of the joint faces, so that the chosen finish will not prevent glueing and apply the finish.

CRAMP TWO SIDES

25 Remove the masking tape. Assemble the two side frames dry, without glue, and test that all joints close. ▼

26 Check that the frame is square and flat. Check internal angles with a try square. ▼

27 Measure the diagonals to check they are identical. If all is well, apply adhesive and cramp with sash cramps, using small blocks of wood between the outside of the legs and the cramp faces to prevent damage. ▲

CHECKING FOR SQUARE

28 It is vital at this stage to check again to ensure that the frame is square and out of winding. If the frame is out of square this can be remedied by adjusting the position of the cramps but the dry assembly should have already shown any problems.

REMOVE EXCESS GLUE

29 When cramping is complete remove the excess glue. Either do this when the glue is wet, using a damp cloth and water, or wait until the glue has cured to a jelly and remove it with a chisel.

If you wait until the glue is hard, damage can be caused to the surfaces around the joints. Also check the mortises and clean out any glue that may prevent the final assembly.

ASSEMBLY OF THE WHOLE FRAME

30 Cramp the whole frame dry again, check that all joints fit, and that the structure is square in all directions. ▼

FURTHER INFORMATION	
70	Holding and cramping
60-61	Finishes

31 This process is slightly more complex than assembling the individual frames, but if you arrange the cramps as shown there should be no problems. ▲

34 Scrape and sand the outside of the frame. ▲

33 When the glue has cured, remove the cramps. Carefully saw off the waste at the top and bottom ends of the legs, and plane these end grain surfaces flat. ▲

32 If all is well dry then disassemble, apply the glue and cramp the frame. Remove excess glue. ▲

35 Check all pre-finished surfaces and apply an overall coat of finish. ▲

MARK OUT THE TOP FRAME

36 The four pieces for the top frame have already been planed square. Mark the mitres at the corners and saw accurately to this line. Glue triangular offcuts to the corners to aid assembly. Then plane the mitres so that all faces fit. You will need to place the frame together and carefully trim the mitres to achieve a perfect fit. ▶

WORK THE REBATE TO HOLD THE CENTRE INSERT

37 This can be done before or after the above process, but *must* be completed before the frame is assembled and glued. The rebate is to be 6mm (¼in) deep so that it can accept a veneered plywood insert, or a sheet of glass or mirror. In later work you will probably use hand power tools (a router) or machine tools to work rebates and grooves, but for this project it is worth using the hand tools, either a rebate or a shoulder plane. ▶

MARK THE DOWEL POSITIONS

38 The top frame could be assembled using tongues or biscuits. For this first piece, dowels are the safest method, since the joint cannot slip when it is being cramped up.

39 Gauge a centre line along each mitre face. Then carefully align the four frame pieces in the vice. Mark the centres of the dowel holes, making a cut line across the four ends to intersect with the gauged centre line on each piece. ▼

40 Mark location points for the dowel drilling using a nail punch. ▼

FURTHER INFORMATION	
70	Holding and cramping
88	Biscuit jointing
118-119	Making dowel joints

41 Drill the holes for the dowels. Ensure that the drill is held upright. ▲

42 Cut the dowels to length. Fit them loose in the holes and cramp the joints dry. You may need to make final adjustments to the mitre faces at this stage.

ASSEMBLY

43 It is possible to use four sash cramps to cramp this frame, and this method works with dowels better than with tongues or biscuits where the joint can slip out of place. A preferable method is to glue triangular offcuts to the outside corners of the joints. ▲

44 When the whole frame is assembled the blocks enable cramping pressure to be applied at right angles to the joint face. ▲

45 If the joint is tight when cramped dry, apply glue and finally cramp. ▼

46 When the glue has cured, remove the cramps and chisel or saw off the triangular blocks. ▶

47 Plane all outside surfaces. ▼

48 Screw the underframe to the top frame. ▶

49 Scrape, sand and finish the frame. ▶

TOP INSERT

50 If you choose glass or mirror, give the glazier a precise cardboard template, since it is very difficult to fit glass that is even slightly oversize.

51 If you decide that you would like an insert with a wood finish, cut a piece of 6mm (¼in) ply, with veneer applied to one face. ▼

52 The finished table, a pleasing addition to any setting. ▲

FURTHER INFORMATION	
47	Preparing the surface
71	Finishing
146-147	Laying veneer

Making a Mortise and Tenon Joint

There are many different mortise and tenon joints, each suitable for a specific purpose. Along with the dovetail joint, the mortise and tenon is one of the most common joints found in woodwork. Practice making the joint before you begin work on an actual project.

The standard stop mortise and tenon joint (shown above) is described on these pages. In the project sections there will be examples of how this basic joint is adapted for specific purposes.

The wood

For this practice exercise, take two pieces of wood (which can be softwood, or an easily worked hardwood) each measuring approximately 250mm (10in) long by 50mm (2in) wide by 20mm (¾in) thick (shown above).

Both pieces of wood must be finished smooth with flat surfaces and edges that are square. The ends should be square also.

Plane the first face true and flat, plane the edge flat and square, mark these with the face and edge marks and finally plane to width and thickness then square both ends.

MARKING OUT THE JOINT

1 Set the mortise gauge precisely to the mortise chisel. However, do all the marking out with a pencil first, and check your marking before you make the final cutting marks with the marking knife or mortise gauge. ▼

2 On the face edge of the piece of wood that is to contain the mortise, or hole, mark the width of the tenon piece, i.e. 50mm (2in), using a pencil and a square. Then as a guide, mark at right angles down the face side and the reverse side. This shows where the tenon will fit. ▼

3 It is usually a good idea to make the tenon with shoulders all round, so put a further set of marks 3mm (⅛in) inside the lines you marked first. ▲

4 As a check that the mortise falls in the centre of the piece of wood, turn the mortise gauge around, place the stock against the other side and see if the pin marks coincide. If they do not, re-adjust the stock until they do. ▶

5 With a mortise gauge, hold the stock firmly against the face side, and mark the two parallel lines for the mortise in the centre of the wood. ▶

8 Take up the tenon piece. The length of the tenon will be equal to the depth of the mortise. Mark all round the tenon, 38mm (1½in) from the end. Use the marking knife for this as you will be sawing from these marks. ▶

6 Mark the precise depth of the mortise in pencil on the face side. Make this mortise 38mm (1½in) deep. ▲

7 With the knife, make two cut lines over the pencil marks on the face edge where the mortise will end. As a general rule use the pencil for guidance marks and cut or gauged lines when you will saw or chisel to that line. ▶

9 With the mortise gauge at the same setting, and with the stock held against the face side, firstly gauge around the face edge and the end. Hold the other end of the wood in the vice to do this. ▲

10 Turn the wood in the vice so that you can gauge the other edge, again with the stock of the mortise gauge held against the face side. ▶

11 With the marking gauge set to 3mm (⅛in) mark the tenon edge shoulders. ▼

FURTHER INFORMATION	
9	Safety first
24-25	Planing
26	Chiselling
26-27	Sawing
34-43	Module 1: small table

CUTTING THE MORTISE

There are several ways to cut a mortise, the method given here is one of the simplest.

1 Hold the mortise piece securely on the bench, or in the vice, well-packed with waste wood. Hold the chisel vertically, locating it within the guidelines and chop across the grain to a depth of 3mm (⅛in), every 3mm (⅛in) or so. Do not chop right up to the end of the mortise for the moment. ▲

2 You will find now that the chopped bits of wood should chisel out very easily from between the gauged lines.

Repeat this procedure, chopping down about 3mm (⅛in) each time, until you have reached a depth of around 38mm (1½in). A piece of masking tape around the chisel blade, 38mm (1½in) from the end, will help guide you. ▲

3 When you have reached the required depth, work up to the cut line to finish off the ends of the mortise. You should now have a mortise hole that is the required width for the tenon. ▲

CUTTING THE TENON

1 Hold the tenon piece in the vice, and with the tenon saw, saw down the gauged lines to the knife cut. Stop about 1mm (1/32in) short of this knife-cut shoulder line. Remember to saw on the waste side of the wood. ▶

2 Saw at an angle of 45° down across the front of the tenon.

3 Then saw down across the back.

4 Saw down to the shoulder.

5 Turn the wood around and repeat the operation on the other 3mm (⅛in) lines.

6 Hold the tenon piece against the bench hook and saw down the shoulder on each of the four sides to a depth of no more than 3mm (⅛in). ▶

7 Put the wood back in the vice and saw down the two 3mm (⅛in) edge shoulders. This reduces the tenon to the length of the mortise. ▶

8 Finally, return to the other shoulder lines and saw the waste pieces off. Check very carefully that you do not go too far. You should now have a sawn tenon that fits into the chiselled mortise. ▼

9 Fit the tenon into the mortise and cramp up the pieces, the shoulders of the tenon should fit precisely up to the face edge of the mortise piece. A skilled woodworker would fit the tenon straight from the saw, but in the early stages you will probably have to make some modifications with a chisel. ▼

Preparing the Surface

Before adding a finish to a project, the whole surface must be flat and smooth. It is sometimes possible for an expert to produce a surface with a plane, but normally, you will need to use other tools and techniques to achieve a smooth, even surface, particularly on timbers which have interlocking grain or other surface difficulties.

1 Hold the scraper in both hands, thumbs towards you. Grip the scraper so that you are bending it into a slight curve away from you. If the corners of the scraper start to dig into the wood, increase the curve slightly. ▲

HOW TO USE A SCRAPER

Using a scraper to finish hardwoods requires practice. The aim is to take a very thin shaving, if you start producing dust and not shavings, then the scraper is blunt and needs re-sharpening. This process generates heat in the metal of the scraper – be warned, your thumbs can get quite sore.

2 Start with the scraper vertical, then tilt it away from you until the burred edge is brought into contact with the wood. Push the scraper away from you to take a thin shaving. ▲

HOW TO USE A SANDING BLOCK

Always take the trouble to use a sanding block when sanding by hand. However hard you try, if you simply use the paper in your hand, you will cause your smoothly planed or scraped surface to develop irregularities, and this will show up on the final finish.

A cork sanding block is firm, but slightly resilient, in a convenient size to fit the hand.

1 Standard-sized sheets of abrasive papers can be torn into quarters to fit around a sanding block. Tear the paper against an edge, such as the work bench. ▲

2 Hold the paper tightly around the block, with the chamfers on top. ▶

3 Always rub the paper along the grain and never across it. Sanding across the grain will create minute scratches on the surface which will be difficult to remove, and these will often show when the final finish is applied. ▲

Tables

The classic mortise and tenon underframe used for the Small Table in Module 1 can form the basis for many other designs. Using the same construction, but changing the size, you can make anything from coffee tables to family-size kitchen or dining tables.

A taller table becomes a pedestal for displaying plants or other objects.

The choice of wood and finishes also contributes to the design. Ash, maple, oak or beech are all suitable choices for a modern table of any size. The surface can also be stained or finished with paint or lacquer.

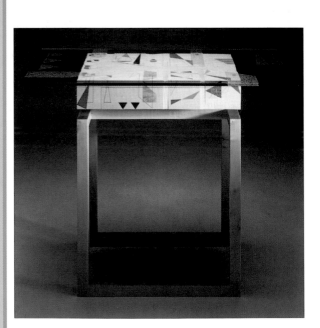

NIC PRYKE • Table
A very simple structure, given added dimension and lift by the inlay decoration on the top unit and the contrast with the extension and the sides. This decoration is appropriate to the piece and besides being a fine piece of inlay work, gives the table an interest and character that makes for an individual piece of visual quality. ▲

ERGONOMICS

Tables for eating or working need to be designed so that they can be used comfortably and without strain. You need to be able to pull up a chair without banging knees or feet, and to have enough elbow room to eat without obstructing someone next to you.

Ergonomics is the study of how human bodies relate to their environment, and this science has provided optimum measurements for furniture to suit people of average height and build.

Table height

Most adults are comfortably seated at a height of 430mm (1ft 5in). The optimum table height for working or eating is 700mm (2ft 4in), while at least 610mm (2ft) of leg room is necessary between the rail and the floor.

700mm (2ft 4in)
610mm (2ft)
430mm (1ft 5in)

IDEAL TABLE HEIGHT
The ideal table height is 700mm (2ft 4in); ideal leg room is 610mm (2ft); ideal seating height is 430mm (1ft 5in).

Place settings
To eat in comfort, the average adult needs an area of table measuring 610mm (2ft) wide by 300mm (1ft) deep. ▶

300mm (1ft)
610mm (2ft)

Whatever the shape of a dining table, the designer must allow sufficient space for the people it is intended to seat. ▶

Round tables can be an especially economical way of seating people in a small space. A table of only 1m (3ft 3in) diameter will seat four people comfortably. Increase the diameter to only 1200m (4ft) to seat six, and to 1.5m (5ft) to seat eight people. ▶

Diameter = 1.2m (4ft)

TYPES OF TABLE

The underframe can be designed with solid wood legs or panel ends in manmade materials, or with a central crossrail and two endframes as in the refectory table (below).

Table tops can be made with a mitred frame. Solid tops are traditionally made of boards joined together with tongue and grooves or dowels. Nowadays biscuit joints are often used.

Furniture designers have devoted much time to solving the problem of how to increase or reduce the size of a tabletop, to suit different occasions. Dropleaf tables need some form of support, as with gateleg and Pembroke tables. There are various styles of draw-leaf table, where the top slides apart. Extra leaves may be hinged upwards, or slotted in. The hinge and pivot design has a double top, which pivots on one corner and then opens up to double its size. This top should be made of manmade board for stability. A tilting top is a traditional design, suitable for occasional or small dining tables.

NIC PRYKE • Dining table
The low view of the photograph gives the table great dramatic qualities. The contrast between timber, glass and metal works very well and the engineering and honest approach to structure make a very positive statement. ▲

Frame

Panel ends

Refectory

Gate-leg underframe with drop-leaf top.

Pembroke

Draw-leaf table with loose leaf or integral folding leaf.

Hinge and pivot

Tilt top

FURTHER INFORMATION	
34-43	Module 1: small table

Advanced Hand Tools

As your skills develop and you undertake more complex projects, the basic tool kit will need to be supplemented.

If you decide to purchase power hand tools or machine tools, a few of the tools shown here will not be necessary, for example, the work of the rebate plane and the hand router will be done by a power router, the bowsaw will be covered by the bandsaw and the panel or keyhole saw will be covered by power jigsaw or fretsaw.

Other specialized tools will be necessary, and the best policy is to buy them as and when they are needed. In this way you will build up a very comprehensive collection.

recesses. It is useful before you proceed to a power router. It often saves time in setting up the power router.

1 Rebate plane
The rebate plane blade extends across the width of the sole. It can plane wide rebates as well as narrow ones. It has no fence or guide, so rebates must be started against a batten nailed or clamped to the work.

2 Block plane
A small, lightweight bench plane, the block plane is used onehanded for planing end grain, chamfers and delicate work. Add extra pressure when required, by placing your other hand over the toe. The blade is set at a shallower angle than other bench planes, and is fitted with the bevel upwards.

3 Shoulder plane
The shoulder plane can be used like the rebate plane, but is most useful when working long mitres on secret mitre dovetails planing shoulders or other fine work.

4 Hand router
This smooths, cuts and cleans up grooves and

Some of this tool's work can be accomplished with the hand router.

5 Router bits
The bits are set at a shallow angle and work with a paring action. The range of bits available makes a versatile tool.

6 Band or web cramps
The band or web cramp consists of a length of nylon webbing tensioned by a ratchet mechanism. It applies equal pressure on all corners and is useful where sash cramps are too heavy or awkward, for example, in gluing frames with mitred corners, particularly small picture frames, and often in chair making.

7 Edging cramp
The edging cramp is a small G-cramp with an extra screw and tommy bar. It is used when applying lippings to a surface, the side pressure pad pushes the lipping tightly home. However, for this to be really useful, quite a number are needed.

8 Sliding bevel
This is invaluable for any angle other than 90 degrees or 45 degrees. It can mark or check both internal and external angles. Set the slotted blade against a protractor or the work. In some projects in this book it is used to mark dovetails instead of a dovetail template.

9 Vernier gauge
A vernier gauge is useful for many measuring tasks. You do not need an expensive engineer's gauge, the small plastic variety with a dial is sufficient. As your work progresses, you will find you reach the level of accuracy required for this tool.

10 Bowsaw
The bowsaw cuts curves and is strong enough to cut quite thick timber. If you do not have power hand tools a bowsaw is the only way of cutting large curved work. It is difficult to use and needs some practice and great care in cutting to the line.

11 Gents or bead saw
The gents or bead saw is extremely useful where a fine cutting line is needed, even though a dovetail saw is often suitable. The fine teeth leave a very smooth finish.

12 Pad or keyhole saw
The pad or keyhole saw was originally used to cut keyholes. A power jigsaw or fretsaw can do the job of cutting holes away from an edge, but there are often times when it is more useful to use this little saw. Drill a hole first in which to start the cut.

FURTHER INFORMATION	
9	Safety first
16-19	Basic hand tools
20-23	Tool maintenance

13 Cutting gauge

A cutting gauge is similar to a marking gauge except instead of a point, a blade is inserted in the end. Use it for marking across the grain, parallel to an edge. It is also useful for cutting veneer. The blade can be removed and sharpened.

14 Carver's mallet

This is a most useful tool both for making joints and for assembly. The round head allows it to strike at any angle. Whenever possible, use a piece of waste wood between the furniture and the mallet to protect the surface.

15 Claw hammer

A good general purpose tool where you need the weight of a heavier hammer but with more direction than a mallet. Most furniture making should only need a pin hammer but there are times when something heavier is needed. The claw is designed to extract nails.

16 Nail punch

A nail punch is used to drive pins and nails below the surface of the timber. The point diameter should be slightly smaller than the nail head. A nail punch can often be used with a pin hammer but there may be occasions when you will need to use a claw hammer.

17 Firmer or out-cannel gouge

Used to make cuts which are not square, this gouge is sharpened on the outside of the curve with the cutting edge on the inside of the curve. This is used to scoop out hollows or grooves.

18 The scribing or in-cannel gouge

This is used for trimming curved shoulders.

19 Slip stone

A slip stone is necessary to sharpen the curved blades of gouges. Its curved profile

23 Rasps

The rasp is a coarse file, it removes wood quickly and leaves a rough surface which is smoothed by a file. These too are used for shaping, and particularly for chairmaking. A range of different types and sizes are illustrated. All are useful but a favourite for many jobs is the circular or rat-tail shape, both file and rasp.

24 Riffler files

Riffler files have shaped ends in many different configurations and they are often the only tools which will enable you to cut into very awkward places in shaped work. You can buy them with rasp heads at one end and file heads at the other.

22 Spokeshaves

Spokeshaves are made to smooth either internal or external curves. External curves can often be cut with a plane or chisel, whereas internal curves can only be smoothed by the spokeshave. The blade is set by the two fine screws. A well-sharpened spokeshave can leave a finish on hardwoods that needs no sanding.

It will take time to get used to this tool so that you take clean cuts and the blade does not chatter or jump.

The craftsman of old would often make his own spokeshave, making the handle to fit a bought blade. If you get the chance to buy a spokeshave blade, do so, and experiment with it. The homemade spokeshave is often superior to the metal tool.

20 The pump action or spiral ratchet screwdriver

This saves time and effort when a lot of screws have to be inserted. It works via straight pressure on the handle or can be used closed to work like an ordinary screwdriver. When using the pump action, always hold the chuck to prevent it slipping.

21 Chuck bit

Chuck bits come in a range of sizes.

enables you to work on the inside faces of a gouge. Most other sharpening can be done on a combination oilstone.

FURTHER INFORMATION	
9	Safety first
16-19	Basic hand tools
20-23	Tool maintenance

Workshop Planning

Wherever you begin woodworking you will want to develop a workshop dedicated to the task of making furniture. You need to consider environmental factors such as heat, ventilation and light, also the layout of the bench and machines, and access for material in and furniture out. A small workshop cannot have dedicated space for each activity and each space must be used for several tasks.

WORKSHOP PLANNING

Draw a scale plan of your workshop and make cardboard cutouts of the bench and machines. Mark the locations of doors, windows and power points, and experiment to find the best situation for each item.

Manmade board and timber are heavy and take up a lot of space. You will also need to get at fittings and consumables easily.

Each machine needs space around it. Materials must be able to pass through saws and planers unobstructed, and on most other machines the material projects to one side or another. When planning make sure one machine does not foul another.

Incoming material

Timber can be up to 5m (15ft) long and manmade boards are typically 1220mm x 2440mm (4ft x 8ft). Fullsize sheets may have to be cut in your yard or at the suppliers. These materials must be kept in the workshop so they remain dry with even temperature and humidity while they are being made up.

Storage

Finish, fittings, adhesive and other consumables can be stored in well-planned shelves, drawers and cupboards. These are worth the time taken in planning and making them. It is a legal requirement for industry to store finishes outside. If

you do not carry great stocks, bring them into the workshop, but try to put them in a secure, possibly fireproof, cupboard.

Workbench

A sturdy bench is essential. Position it, if possible, in natural light, near a window, if not, good artificial light is necessary.

Hard floor surfaces get very uncomfortable if you

are working for long periods. Lay industrial rubber matting around the work area in front of the bench.

Cutting and assembling

All the projects in this book are relatively small, but the desk and chair need more assembly space than you may think. Leave space for a couple of saw horses so wood can be laid down for chalking and rough cutting, and for assembling cabinets. Consider height

as well as ground area for large items like sideboards, dressers and dining tables.

Finishing

Your choice of finish may have to be influenced by your working environment. If you are using lacquer you must have some means of air extraction, necessary if you are using a brush, but absolutely vital if you are spraying. When using oils, always unfold the cloths and preferably put them

Anatomy of a workshop

1 Finishing room; **2** compressor and spray gun; **3** extractor fan; **4** main entrance; **5** saw horses; **6** manmade boards; **7** small fittings and consumables; **8** timber storage; **9** bandsaw; **10** hand tool storage; **11** workbenches; **12** table saw; **13** planer thicknesser; **14** pillar drill; **15** power hand tools; **16** dust extractor.

outside to dry. Oily cloths left in a bundle can self-ignite.

Dust extraction

When spraying the air must be free of dust. Machining and sanding generate a great deal of dust. If possible, ensure that all machines are connected to a dust extractor. Wear a face mask when spraying or doing dusty jobs.

Light

One of the most important considerations is light. A good source of natural light is best, backed up with carefully placed sources of artificial light. Tungsten light is preferable to fluorescent, with individual spotlights over the workbench and over some of the machines.

Heat

Your workshop should be heated to just under the temperature of the place where the piece of furniture will finally be

situated. Furniture makers working in cold and damp workshops have had work spoilt by timber movement when it has been taken into a centrally heated environment.

Scrap and waste

You will often have small pieces of wood and other materials that can come in handy for subsequent jobs. Anything of a respectable size is worth putting in a special bin where you can get at it easily.

What is not useable

scrap is waste – shavings, sawdust etc. Sweep up daily, since waste on the floor is a potential hazard.

Safety

Keep the work space tidy. Have a fire extinguisher and first-aid box fitted to a wall where they are in plain view of anyone coming into the workshop. Fit a smoke alarm.

Delivery

Make sure you can get finished furniture out of the workshop into the car,

trailer or van and into its final location. Large pieces may need making in sections for final construction or delivery.

FURTHER INFORMATION	
9	Safety first
16-19	Basic hand tools
50-53	Advanced hand tools
76-77	Power hand tools
92-93	Machine tools

PASSAGE OF PIECES THROUGH THE WORKSHOP

For an effective layout look at the processes involved in furniture-making. Materials, finishes and fittings must be brought in. Marking out and cutting need to be near the table saw and planer. Group the bench, machine tools and power hand tool area around the assembly area.
    The finishing area should be separate with provision for air extraction especially if you are using lacquers. Finally, leave room to take finished furniture out.

Store – timber, manmade board, fittings and consumables

Main outside finish store

Mark out and prepare – saw and plane

Bench

Materials in

Furniture out

Machine tools

Assembly area

Finishing

Power hand tools

Principles of Frame Construction

With cabinet and chair construction, the frame is the basis for many pieces of furniture. Some chairs are basic frames, most tables are either open or closed frames (a table with four legs and top rails only is an open frame).

Frames are found in doors, and some cabinets can be based on frame construction. In fact, the idea of frame and panel construction gives a very economical way of making furniture since thin panels are possible that will make light frames quite rigid.

In England during the Second World War Utility furniture was developed to give quality products with very economical use of materials. Unfortunately, its potential was not fully exploited after the War.

FRAME DEVELOPMENT

Early furniture used logs, but as woodworking developed, timber was converted into planks and then into squares or rectangles. Some early furniture is obviously plank derived. However, it was found that strong constructions could be achieved by using timber as vertical and horizontal frame members. Furniture today still follows these basic principles. Some different frame applications are shown on this page.

Chairs

Some early chairs and some very simple modern chairs make use of the frame. The number and width of rails help improve the structure and of course the insertion of a panel will further help, for example in Jacobean panel chairs. ▲

Tables

The table is either a closed or open frame. A small coffee or display table is quite strong at this scale and the top is a great help in keeping the frame square. With dining tables, however, there is always the problem of fitting knees under the top rail and the wish to maximize leg room. ▼

Doors

Doors are one of the most common ways where frames are reinforced by panels. ▲

Cabinets

A cabinet can be made using a light frame and thin panel construction. It is true this is a cheap method of manufacture and is often found in batch furniture, but the principle is sound and good furniture can arise from delicate use of this system. ▼

Built-in furniture

The front frame that holds the doors of large cupboards is a good example of frame construction. It is essential to ensure that when the frame is inserted, there is a means of checking and making it square so that the doors will work properly. ▼

PROBLEMS OF FRAME CONSTRUCTION

The development of the frame gave rise to the mortise and tenon joint but the square or rectangle is not an integrally strong basic structure. In order to make the right angle strong, it needs triangulation and it is this that most forms of construction try to accomplish.

Strengthening methods

One way of strengthening a square frame is to make one or two of the members as deep as possible so one thicker rail holds the whole structure. ▼

On tables, the deep top rail is not there as a visual feature but is often needed to strengthen a long mortise and tenon. As an alternative to a deep rail, the rail may be thickened towards the joint, with a gunstock-shouldered mortise and tenon. ▲

Another, and simpler, way of adding maximum strength is by inserting a panel within the frame. This principle is used in many pieces to solve the problem of right-angled joints. ▶

Another method is a combination of deep rails and panel inserts. Gussets or triangular pieces in the corner of quite a light frame will add enormous strength. In open shelving systems diagonal bracing on the back is often used to serve the same function. ▶

Strengthening right-angle joints

There are two specific solutions to the problem of strengthening a right angle. Traditionally-made chairs have corner blocks in each of the four corners. These of course support a drop-in seat, but their job really is to keep the frame square. ▶

To achieve fine table legs without sacrificing leg room, one way is to reinforce the legs, triangulating them back up to a member across the top. ▼

FURTHER INFORMATION	
32-33	Basic jointing
34-43	Module 1: small table
48-49	Tables

The Principles of Cabinet Construction

Cabinets were traditionally made from solid wood. The wood could be left natural, veneered, polished, stained or lacquered.

During this century advances in manmade board have produced plywood, blockboard, chipboard and MDF. Construction techniques for manmade materials call for a different approach.

CABINETS IN SOLID TIMBER

The main fact to bear in mind is that timber moves. There is hardly any movement along the grain, but a surprising amount of movement across it, and all cabinetmaking techniques using solid wood seek to allow for this.

Cross-grain movement varies with the timber, its moisture content and conditions in which it is used. Controlled heat and humidity tend to stabilize the timber at a particular stage, but changes in moisture and humidity mean the timber will move markedly. It can vary between $1/50$ to $1/100$ of the width, i.e. between 3mm and 6mm ($1/8$in and $1/4$in) in a 300mm (12in) width.

Min ▶ ◀

Max

Timber moves more across the grain than along its length.

All grain works together

Battens are screwed in slots

Carcase construction

By constructing a cabinet with the grain direction running around it, the whole cabinet works together, any movement being from back to front. Battens running across the cabinet, from front to back, cannot simply be glued in place. To allow for timber movement they must be screwed to the sides. Insert one screw in a hole, the other screws in slots. Ensure that the length of this cross batten is reduced so that it will not foul backs or doors. ▲

Panel construction

When fitting solid wood into a frame, the panel must be allowed to move within the groove. Either leave the panel free and do not glue, or put a spot of glue in the centre of the panel so that the sides can move. ▶

Allow frame to move in the groove

Back construction

The same procedure is necessary for backs of cabinets, which can be solid wood or ply. ▼

Cabinet back fitted into grooved frame

Tabletops

The same principle is found in solid table tops where battens are screwed to the underside to keep the top flat. Designer/craftsman Alan Peters cuts this batten in the form of a dovetail which gives a beautiful visual detail in his table. ▼

Slot-screwed battens keep table tops flat

Dovetail detail

Muntin for wide boards

Grain direction in drawers

Drawers

Drawers must also follow this principle on grain direction. Plywood drawer bottoms present no problem, but with solid timber the grain direction should run side to side, with the screws holding the bottom to the back in slots to allow for the movement. ▲

Slot- screw the bottom

MANMADE BOARD

Manmade board is inert and any movement will be in all directions, therefore jointing systems can be much simpler.

Mitred box with tongues or biscuits

KEEPING CABINETS SQUARE

Cabinets must be kept square. Distortion can lead to joints failing and doors and drawers jamming. Corner joints alone are rarely enough to hold a cabinet rigid.

Box base

Strengthening the base

A five-sided box at the base of the cabinet acts in a similar way to the principle of a wide rail in frame construction. If the box is strong and rigid and the sides firmly secured, this will give the whole cabinet rigidity. ▲

Ply or frame and panel back

Strengthening the back

Many cabinet designs rely on the back for rigidity. This can be a sheet of ply sliding into grooves or rebates or a frame and panel. ▲

Strengthening the interior

A cabinet with partition shelves and drawer runners. Grain direction of all pieces must allow for movement of the wood. Runners are slot-screwed in place. ▼

USE OF JOINTS

A range of joints can be used. In solid wood decide whether you want the joint to be decorative and to show. Corner joints can be through dovetails, the partitioning joints can be through multiple mortise and tenons.

If you do not want the joints to show, but want to practice cabinetmaking, use single lap, double lap or secret mitre dovetails for corner joints. Use tapered dovetail housings for partitions. However, as long as you remember to allow for grain movement, the cabinet can be joined with tongues or biscuits.

Manmade boards will be covered with a veneer or paint finish, so all joints can be hidden in the mitre: dowels, tongues or biscuits. Simple butt joints will be glued and pinned or screwed if you wish to finish with filler and paint. Screws or pins must be recessed and covered with filler.

Lapped dovetail

Secret or mitre dovetail

Mitre joint

Finishes

A finish is applied to wood to improve its decorative qualities and to protect it from the elements and from general use. The choice of finish will depend on the nature of the piece you have made, the characteristics of the wood and the situation in which the piece will be used.

There is a wide choice and the decision as to what to use will be made on practical considerations of protection or on how to enhance the appearance of particular timber. With some timbers it is quite suitable to leave the wood without a finish, especially where it is used inside, however, a finish does enhance most timbers.

TYPES OF FINISH

A finish has either a low or high build, or thickness. It is unusual to leave timber completely natural. However, you may wish to use a very low build finish, such as oil or wax. These enhance the nature of the wood, give some protection and allow the natural character of the wood to predominate. However, dirt will easily get into the grain and the pores and the finish will have to be regularly attended to, added to, or sometimes stripped and re-applied from scratch.

You can apply a higher build finish which seals the timber grain but does not completely encapsulate the wood. You can see and feel grain through finish. There are times when you wish to completely fill the grain and apply a high build finish so that you can see the wood colour and pattern but not feel the texture.

A finish can either be matt, satin or high gloss. The higher the gloss required the more build of finish has to be applied, therefore you have to use fillers and several coats of lacquer, sanded between each coat.

Wood can be left without finish. Simply rub very fine wire wool over the wood for a matt surface. For a satin finish use wire wool with wax polish. For a very high build finish use lacquer and burnish it so that it gives a high gloss encapsulation of the wood.

1 Linseed oil
Linseed oil takes several weeks to dry between coats, but the finish is very durable.

2 Tung and Danish oils
Tung and Danish oils have added chemicals to hasten drying.

3 Beeswax
Beeswax is natural wax which needs regular attention if used alone.

4 Paste wax polish
Paste wax polish is generally best applied over a finish and not used alone.

5 Clear lacquer
Clear lacquer can be sprayed or, if thinned, brushed on. May be a one or two-part type.

6 Polyurethane varnish
Polyurethane varnish is a synthetic resin that is easy to apply and hard-wearing.

7 Wood stains
Wood stains are useful if you want to enrich a wood that has

an undistinguished colour (for example, some of the mahoganies) or to use a positive non-timber colour (for example, primary colours).

8 Shellac
Shellac is a constituent of French polish, it gives a beautiful finish, but is damaged by heat and moisture.

9 Brushes
Brushes to apply finishes range from cheap to expensive. All need care in cleaning and storage.

10 Aerosol cans
Aerosol cans are useful for small jobs. They may be cellulose or acrylic but are expensive for large jobs.

11 Cloth and wadding
Cloth and wadding are used to make a rubber to apply French polish and oils.

WOOD TYPES/APPROPRIATE FINISH

You can use any finish on any timber, but some woods lend themselves better to particular finishes.

Fumed oak: Ammonia fumes colour wood containing tannic acid. Oak turns golden to dark brown. Add a clear lacquer finish to protect the colour.

Mahogany – high gloss: Mahogany traditionally has a high build and high gloss finish. It often needs staining to enrich the colour since few mahoganies available today have the depth of colour of Cuban mahogany used in the 18th and 19th centuries.

Oiled teak: Teak's natural properties make it resistant to rot and insect attack and is ideal for an oil finish.

Ash-matt lacquer: Ash has an interesting grain and it is preferable not to add a high build finish. A matt finish is more appropriate.

Waxed walnut: Walnut is a lovely timber which looks good when waxed. With dark woods white waxes are not always appropriate so buy a wax of a darker colour.

Waxed walnut

Wall-Hung Cabinet

The finished appearance of this small wall-hung cabinet is deceptively simple. The cabinet sides are joined to the top and bottom with secret mitre dovetails. The dovetail joint is completely hidden by the mitred shoulders and its construction is a real test of accurate marking and cutting. The back consists of a panel fitted into a grooved mortise and tenon frame.

A rebate cut around its outside edge enables the back frame to slot neatly into a matching groove in the cabinet.

The shelf is tongued into stopped housings cut in the sides. Finally, the completed cabinet is cleverly and neatly suspended from the top rail which is bevelled to locate onto a wall-mounted batten.

AIMS OF THE PROJECT
Introducing secret mitre dovetail joints.
Making a frame and panel construction.
Making stopped housing joints.

TOOLS YOU WILL NEED
Chalk
Pencil
Rule
Panel saw
Marking gauge
Marking knife
Jack plane
Dovetail saw
Range of chisels
Mortise gauge
Try square
Power router or plough plane and a hand router
Sash cramps
Cabinet scraper
Sanding block

TIME TO ALLOW
Allow plenty of time for this project if you are new to woodworking. You will need at least three or four weekends.

REMEMBER
When cultivating new skills such as cutting dovetails, or any joint encountered for the first time, do make one or more samples first, before working on the main timber.

HEALTH AND SAFETY
Follow the safe working procedures outlined on page 9.

CHOOSING WOOD

It is possible to use almost any of the quality furniture-making hardwoods for this project. Choose a wood that is neither too hard nor too soft. Maple, ash or beech would be appropriate from among the light-coloured timbers, mahogany would be a suitable red timber, and walnut a darker choice.

Joinery grade softwood or the hard and brittle softwood, yew, are not recommended as precise, clean cuts are essential for well-fitting joints.

No	Sawn	Planed
CUTTING LIST		
2	SIDES 610mm x 280mm x 25mm 2ft x 11in x 1in	560mm x 250mm x 20mm 1ft 10in x 10in x ¾in
1	TOP 432mm x 280mm x 25mm 1ft 5in x 11in x 1in	380mm x 250mm x 20mm 1ft 3in x 10in x ¾in
1	BOTTOM 432mm x 250mm x 25mm 1ft 5in x 10in x 1in	380mm x 235m x 20mm 1ft 3in x 9¼in x ¾in
1	SHELF 380mm x 250mm x 20mm 1ft 3in x 10in x ¾in	356mm x 230mm x 12mm 1ft 2in x 9in x ½in
2	FOR FRAMED BACK STILES (UPRIGHTS) 610mm x 45mm x 25mm 2ft x 1¾in x 1in	565mm x 38mm x 20mm 1ft 10¼in x 1½in x ¾in
2	RAILS 406mm x 60mm x 25mm 1ft 4in x 2½in x 1in	356mm x 50mm x 22mm 1ft 2in x 2in x ⅞in
1	WALL BATTEN 305mm x 45mm x 12mm 12in x 1¾in x ½in	280mm x 35mm x 10mm 11in x 1⅜in x ⅜in
1	BACK PANEL manmade board approx. 480mm x 305mm x 6mm 1ft 7in x 12in x ¼in	

+ masking tape, finishing, adhesive, 2 screws for cabinet back, wall fixings for batten

PLANS

The drawings on this page show the elevations and sections, together with an exploded perspective view of the finished piece.

Scale 1:9

Back slides up from bottom in grooves on sides and top

Exploded diagram

← 380mm 1′3″ →

Sectional half plan through A-A

20mm 3/4″

240mm 9½″

12mm ½″

265mm 10½″

20mm 3/4″

A ---- A

Centre line

560mm 1′10″

Front elevation

250mm 10″

Sectional side elevation through centre line

20mm 3/4″

6mm ¼″

50mm 2″

35mm 1⅜″

6mm ¼″

25mm 1″

Front elevation at X

Wall batten

7mm 5/16″

50mm 2″

6mm ¼″

Sectional rear detail at Z

22mm 7/8″

FURTHER INFORMATION	
24-25	Planing
30-31	Reading drawings
32-33	Basic jointing
58-59	Principles of cabinet construction
68-69	Making dovetail joints

TIMBER PURCHASE

1 Most of the timber for this job could be prepared from 25mm (1in) thick sawn board.

2 Mark out all the components on the board in chalk and carefully saw them.

PLANING ALL COMPONENTS

3 Plane the face sides and face edges. Apply face and edge markings. Gauge and plane to width, then gauge and plane the thickness.

MARK OUT THE CABINET

4 Mark out the main cabinet parts, the two sides, the top and the bottom. You will see from the drawing that the bottom is slightly narrower than the other three components since the back will slide up in a groove from the bottom of the cabinet.

5 Mark overall and shoulder lengths in pencil. Mark the shelf position. Check all marking before you begin any cutting.

6 Work the grooves in the sides and top to accommodate the back panel. This will be an easy job if you have a router, or use a plough plane. ▲

CORNER JOINTS

7 The joints on this cabinet could be either mitres using dowels, tongues or biscuits, or dovetails using through dovetails, single lap, double lap or secret mitre. For this project, "bite the bullet" and make a secret mitre dovetail. It is important that you practise this joint on a spare piece of wood before committing yourself to the main carcase.

8 Pay particular attention when marking out to the junction between the two sides and the bottom at the back, because instead of a mitre in this position, the sides must be kept square.

9 Mark the shoulders on the inside faces. Mark the mitre on the edges. You must remove timber from both parts of the joint in the form of a rebate across the end. The timber that is left represents the dovetail pins and tails. As is normal practice, the dovetails will be on the sides and the pins on the top and bottom.

10 Mark and cut the pins first. Mark the dovetail pins on the two components, at the ends of the top and the bottom. ▼

11 Cut the pins and remove the waste by a series of saw cuts and by paring with a chisel. ▼

12 Mark the tails on to the sides but before doing so letter or number each joint clearly. Working on one joint at a time, mark the precise position of the tails from the pins. Be sure to hatch in the waste that you wish to remove. ▼

13 Remove the waste from between the tails, using a dovetail saw and chisel.

14 The lap dovetails on the bottom corners can now be tapped together, the dovetails on the secret mitre will only fit partially together, but you can check and adjust at this stage. ▼

15 The secret mitre joints will not come tightly together until you have cut the mitre on the front faces, on the rear faces and across the corner. When this mitre is cut you should be able to tap the dovetail home. ▶

16 Assemble the cabinet dry at this stage and check that the joints fit. ▲

SHELF

17 The total length of the shelf includes the housing depth. Mark in pencil a 6mm (¼in) shoulder all round both ends of the shelf. Check that the shoulder lines are precisely the width of the shoulders on top and bottom. ▼

18 Now saw the shoulders and finish with the shoulder plane. ▼

19 Disassemble the cabinet and mark the housings, first in pencil, then with cut lines. In this first job it is advisable to have a shoulder all round, even though housings can be made bare-faced or with a dovetail on one edge.

FURTHER INFORMATION	
70	Holding and cramping
86-87	Using a router

20 Cut the housings in the sides. Check the shoulder length and mark and cut the tongues to fit the housings. ▼

21 Again, reassemble the whole carcase dry and check it for square at the corners and diagonally, both front and back. ▼

22 Apply sash cramps to determine the best sequence for assembly. Generally with this type of cabinet joint you should only need to clamp the tails into the pins from side to side.

23 Disassemble, clean up the insides of the cabinet and all round the shelf, mask the joint surfaces where they will be glued and apply a finish to the inside.

24 Remove the masking tape from the joints, apply the glue and cramp the carcase, remembering to check again for square.

25 When the glue has cured, sand the outside of the carcase and apply the required finish. ▼

BACK FRAME

26 Mark out the back components. This is a simple frame with mortise and tenon joints at the four corners. Since the frame is grooved to hold the ply panel, the haunches on the tenons are square, rather than sloping as on the Small Table, so that they fill the groove. ▼

27 Cut the groove for the ply panel on the inside of the frame components using a router. Notice that the top rail is thicker than the two stiles. This is so that the cabinet carcase will be held away from the wall when the top rail is located on the wall-mounted batten. ▶

28 Mark and plane the bevel on the top rail where the support batten will fit. When marking remember that the extra thickness is on the outside of the back frame, refer to the full-size detail drawing for clarity, and double check all marking out before cutting.

29 Cut the mortises and haunched tenons, having first checked your marking yet again.

30 Mark the back panel out on the plysheet. Check your marking, cut and fit the panel into the back frame. Assemble the frame and panel dry, cramp and check for square.

31 The back frame has a rebate cut around the outer edge which enables it to slide into the back of the cabinet. Work this rebate now. ▼

32 If all is well, glue up the back, checking it for square and wind. Remove the cramps when the glue has cured. Then check that the back slides into the cabinet. ▲

33 Finish all components on both cabinet and back. Slide the back into place from the bottom upwards. Remember to have the bevelled rail at the top of the cabinet. Fix the back in the cabinet with two screws at the bottom. ▼

34 Make the wall batten, and plane the bevel to fit the top rail. Fit the batten to the wall. ▼

35 The finished cabinet brings together a number of classic cabinet-making techniques. ▶

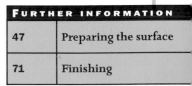

FURTHER INFORMATION	
47	Preparing the surface
71	Finishing

Making Dovetail Joints

For many furniture makers the dovetail is a pleasurable joint to make since it is both decorative and a display of skill. It holds two pieces of timber together, normally at a cabinet or drawer corner. One part of a dovetail joint consists of the tails and the other part the pins. There are other ways of making corner joints as described below, but the through dovetail joint is a real demonstration of a woodworker's skill, and this is the joint shown in this technique.

Dovetail proportions are generally judged by eye to give a balanced and attractive result. Note the arrangement of pins and tails on narrow rails or wide boards. Draw the proportions of the dovetails on a piece of paper, then decide which to make first: the pins or the tails. For through dovetails, either way is acceptable but when you begin making laps, double laps and secret mitres it is much easier to make the pins first and mark the tails from them, so this system is used here.

Preparation

There are two methods of working: either make the dovetails exactly to the correct length or make them so that the pins and tails project past the face of the wood, which is then planed down. The best method is to make the joint to the correct length from the first, as this is necessary in several applications shown later. Prepare the two pieces of timber, exactly planing the face side, face edge, marking them and then planing width and thickness and carefully squaring both ends.

The wood

The through dovetail is generally used for the corners of cabinets, boxes or drawers, so any conveniently sized softwood will do. Two pieces of timber 200mm (8in) long by 100mm (4in) wide by 20mm (¾in) thick will be suitable.

Proportions

Different ways of arranging dovetail proportions are shown below. Generally the pins are finer than the tails. Angles must not be too great, leaving short grain on tails, nor too shallow to be effective.

Types of dovetail
1   Even spacing.
2   Tails grouped at the sides.
3   Decorative and functional.
4   Too much slope.
5   Too little slope.

MARKING THE PINS

1 Set the cutting gauge to the thickness of the wood and then gauge around one end of each piece from the end to mark the shoulder line. ▶

2 Put one piece in the vice gauged end uppermost. Using a sliding bevel, mark out the pins in pencil, and shade in the waste to be removed. When you are sure you have it right in pencil, mark cut lines on the end surface with a knife. Later, if you make many dovetail joints, you may make or buy a dovetail template. ▶

3 Using a square and marking knife, mark down from the end of the dovetail lines. ▶

CUTTING THE PINS

1 With a dovetail saw, carefully saw to the waste side of the line following down to the shoulder line. ▶

2 Saw out the waste with a coping saw, making sure the saw cut is about 1.5mm (¹⁄₁₆in) from the shoulder line. ▼

3 Pare down to the shoulder at the gauge line working from each side so as not to split the surface of the wood. There should now be a series of nice crisp "holes" for which you have to make some tails. ▶

MARKING TAILS FROM THE PINS

1 Lay the piece of wood which is to have the tails on the bench face side up, and place the piece already cut in the position in which it is to fit. Putting the marking knife against the side of the pin, make a cut line. ▼

2 Shade the waste areas. Check here that you have marked this correctly and then, using a square and a knife, take the lines across the end of the wood. ▼

CUTTING THE TAILS

1 The procedure is similar to cutting the pins. Saw to the waste side of the line down to the shoulder line. ▲

2 Now saw out the waste with a coping saw and, as previously, chisel to the shoulder line. ▲

FITTING THE TWO PARTS

1 The joint should fit first time. However, as this is a first attempt, put the piece with the pins in the vice, pins uppermost, and place the piece with the tails in position. Protecting the outside of the wood with a piece of waste, tap the joint together for about 3mm (¹⁄₈in) with a hammer. ▼

2 See how the joint is fitting and decide if any chiselling is necessary to make the joint fit. The interference between any two parts will show when the joint is taken apart. Pare carefully, making sure you do not take out too much, and fit the joint which should now be able to be tapped home.

FURTHER INFORMATION	
9	Safety first
62-67	Module 2: wall-hung cabinet

Holding and Cramping

When you use any cramps, always make sure the face of the work is protected by using a small pad of waste wood under the cramp faces. It is often convenient to fix these protective blocks in place on the clamp heads with masking or double-sided tape first.

To make a wide board from narrower lengths use sash cramps to exert pressure on the joint, positioning them on both sides of the board.

1 Lay the bottom cramps on the bench, glue and gently pinch the joints. Wipe away any excess glue squeezed out of the joints. ▲

2 Locate the upper cramps and tighten all cramps. This will ensure that the board does not spring, but stays flat. Such surfaces can be glued only, or you can use dowels, tongue and groove or biscuit joints. ▲

CRAMPING A FRAME

1 Sash cramps ensure joints are tight when cramping a frame. Check the frame is not in wind or twist by sighting from rail to rail, from stile to stile or leg to leg. ▼

2 Check the frame is square by using a try square and by checking the diagonals. If the frame is out of square, move the cramps as shown to correct it. ▼

CRAMPING A MITRE

There are two methods. Use four sash cramps and tighten very carefully to ensure the mitre closes. This method is fine when the mitre is dowelled since the joint cannot slip.

However, if tongues or biscuits are used, slipping can cause problems and the alternative method is better. Glue softwood triangular cheeks to the outside of the frame corners (shown above). This enables the cramps to apply pressure all along the joint.

When the glue is cured, saw off the cheeks and plane the edges. ▲

CRAMPING A CABINET

The principles of cramping and checking are similar to those applied when cramping a frame. The operation can be very complex, however, requiring many cramps.

It is essential that cabinet assembly is carefully planned and that you have a dry run without glue first, before the final assembly with glue.

USING A SASH CRAMP IN A VICE

Grip the sash cramp in the vice, using packing blocks each side of the cramp. Use this technique to hold long work, or for example, when planing square timber to a cylinder or making facetted (hexagonal or octagonal) components. ▼

Finishing

The finishes available are summarized earlier on in this book. You must first decide which finish is appropriate to the completed work. This decision depends upon the nature of the piece and how and where it is to be used. For table surfaces a hard lacquer may be best but on certain chairs oil is preferable. Before applying any of the finishes discussed below the timber surfaces must be well prepared by planing, scraping and sanding.

APPLYING OIL WITH A CLOTH

Using a clean, soft cloth folded into a pad, wipe the oil on the timber. Do not over-apply. The surface should not be swimming in oil, any oil that has not been taken into the pores should be wiped off after a few minutes.

Apply a series of light coats rather than heavy ones. Oil is a finish that needs time to build up. There is a saying: "apply once a day for a week, once a week for a month and once a month for a year". ▶

APPLYING ONE-PART LACQUER WITH A BRUSH

Do not attempt to apply thick coats, but brush the lacquer on thinly and allow it to soak into the grain (shown above). When the lacquer has hardened cut it down with fine silicon carbide paper. Work through the grades of paper to the very finest available. Make sure the surface is dust-free before continuing with applications of lacquer. Finally apply a coat of wax polish and buff to a sheen. ▲

APPLYING TWO-PART LACQUER WITH A MOP

1 Mix the hardener (catalyst) with the lacquer to the proportions recommended by the manufacturer, usually one part of catalyst to nine parts lacquer. ▶

2 Mix only enough for the work in hand since any left over becomes like jelly and then hard and cannot be used. Apply thin coats of lacquer with a mop. Cut down between each coat as described above for one-part lacquers. Subsequent applications will build to a good hard-wearing finish. ▶

3 After the final application, for a "satin" finish, apply a wax coating (see "Applying wax", right) or, for a high gloss finish, the surface can be burnished either by mechanical buffing or by using automotive burnishing paste. ▶

MAKING A HOLDER FOR A MOP

A mop is an expensive and specialized tool, and many furniture makers make a holder specially for it from a glass jar with a metal screw top filled with lacquer thinner or cleaner. Cut a hole in the metal top and push the handle through so the bristles are suspended in the thinner. This keeps the mop in good condition and always ready for use. ▼

APPLYING WAX

Wax is best as a final finish for oils or lacquers. Apply the wax with a cloth, or with the finest grade of wire wool in a very thin film. Leave for a while then buff with a soft dry cloth.

FURTHER INFORMATION	
9	Safety first
60-61	Finishes

Cabinet

The basic cabinet consisting of four sides and a back can be varied in many ways. Solid wood sides joined with dovetails is the classic traditional method shown in Module 2.

Joints can be hidden, or they can be visible, contributing to the appeal of the finished piece. The carcase can be of solid wood, or a frame and panel construction as used for the desk in Module 6. Manmade board can be used and combined with modern machine jointing methods.

SHAPE AND SIZE

Cabinets can be made in a variety of different shapes and sizes, depending on what they will hold, and the space available. Large cabinets stand on the floor to become bookcases or cupboards.

A cabinet can also be combined with other furniture – standing on a table, for example. Cabinets of different proportions may also be combined to make more elaborate pieces of furniture such as dressers, or wardrobes.

A wall-hung cabinet, if it is to carry heavy loads, must be securely fixed. You can give extra support by screwing a batten to the wall for the cabinet to rest on, as well as hanging the cabinet from the top.

Floor-standing cabinet

Wall-hung cabinet

LEE SINCLAIR • *Shelving screen*

Made in painted MDF and ash, this clever combination of a screen and shelves gives an added dimension to a room divider. The panels were decorated by Cynthia Harrison using acrylic paint then sealed with clear lacquer. ▲

Proportion

Make a scale drawing of the front elevation to consider variations in the proportion of your cabinet designs. The shape should look right in terms of proportion and balance, and you can also use the drawing to check that the cabinet will hold all the objects you want to store.

A long design may need extra support in the middle.

A tall design may not be stable, and may need fixing to the wall, even if it is floor-standing. ▶

Inside the cabinet

A cabinet interior can be arranged in many different ways too. Shelves can be varied in number and proportion, or they can be combined with drawers. ▼

Shelves can be fixed or adjustable. Adjustable shelves increase the versatility of the cabinet. It will improve the rigidity of the cabinet if at least one central shelf is fixed. ▼

A display cabinet, where the pattern of the shelves forms an important part of the design, calls for careful planning. The shelves could be made from a contrasting wood to the outer carcase. ▼

DOORS

A door or doors can be added to the cabinet, or you could choose to include some areas of open shelving. Doors can be made using a frame and panel to allow for movement in the wood. With manmade boards, doors can be fitted as a single sheet.

A single door opening on a simple hinge is the most basic form. ▼

Double hinged doors are hinged in the same way, but the central break down the front of the cabinet creates a very different look. ▼

Sliding doors must run in grooves inside the cabinet. These can either be routed out, or you can buy pre-formed plastic sections to screw into the cabinet. For large or heavy doors buy a specially-made roller mechanism combined with track and glide mechanism for the bottom of the door. Sliding doors are useful in a restricted space, but only half the cabinet is accessible at any one time. ▼

Fold and slide doors allow access to the whole of the cabinet interior. The doors must be mounted on a proprietary roller-guide system. ▼

Open and fold away doors need compartments at the side with enough room to take each door. ▼

Vertical folding doors including rise and fold and fall flap doors require specialist hardware. Before you consider a design using these features, check that you can buy the required hinges and stays. ▼

Instead of doors, for an entirely different design approach use a paper screen, roller blind or slat blind to cover the front of a cabinet. ▼

Paper screen   Roller blind   Slat blind

NIC PRYKE ● *Display case*
This elegant piece for displaying objects was specially commissioned by a museum. The delicately tapering oak legs are bleached and sandblasted. The patinated copper shelves have been subjected to heat and a chemical process which causes the coloration. ◄

These projects take you further into furniture-making. Module Three, nursery furniture, introduces the techniques used in working manmade board. It is easier to use than solid timber, but the basic skills covered earlier are essential: planning and marking accurately. You will easily be able to adapt the use of this material to your own designs. Module Four, the small chest, introduces drawer making and includes a variation on cabinet construction, using machine joints. Drawer making is a very good combination of skills and you will use this again in other jobs. This section also introduces chair making with a simple but original design using shaped solid timber to give interest on the seat and back. The chair has joints that show and add to the effect of the entire piece. On completion of these modules your skills will have developed well, giving you a springboard to more complex projects.

Power Hand Tools

Even though it is important to develop a feel for wood by using hand tools, their machine equivalents are immensely valuable. Power hand tools are not only useful for removing the drudgery of routine tasks, but results can often be achieved much more quickly and easily than by hand. The router and biscuit jointer particularly are the power tools that really give the ability to carry out work that would otherwise require a lot of skill and specialist hand tools. You must, however, always follow all the safety rules when using these tools.

1 Circular saw

The circular saw can cut either along or across the grain and can be used as a machine held in the hand or inverted on a specially-designed frame to make a miniature table saw. Always take great care to ensure that it is fully guarded at all times and that you are very methodical in its operation.

2 Jigsaw

One of the first power tools to buy, since it is so versatile. It can make straight cuts with or across the grain and also free-shaped cuts. It is good for jobs ranging from timber conversion to quite substantial shaping work. Initially, it is a good stand-in for a bandsaw and a fretsaw. With care it can cut timber up to 50mm (2in) thick. It can accept a variety of blades, and even cut thin metal sheet and plastic laminate.

3 Router

The router can do so many jobs, from simply cutting grooves and rebates to a wide range of small moulding operations, using some of the many specialist cutters available. There are also specialist jigs which allow the router to perform as a dovetail machine. Once you have become familiar with the machine, you will find its only limitation is your imagination.

4 Router cutters

Router cutters are either high speed steel (HSS) or the longer lasting tungsten carbide tipped (TCT). Shank diameters are 6.38mm (¼in), 9mm (⅜in) or 12mm (½in).

5 Belt sander

A very effective tool, but needs care as it can ruin fine

10 Battery pack and charger
More and more tools are battery rather than mains powered. Recent advances in technology have seen the rates at which battery chargers operate fall from 16 hours to 5 minutes.

work by taking off too much timber. It is preferable to use the plane, the scraper and abrasive paper. The belt sander, however, is useful inverted in a stand where it can be used for sanding and shaping small items.

6 Drill
Probably the oldest of the electric tools, long used by DIY enthusiasts. It is preferable to have at least a couple in different sizes, one small battery powered machine for fine work and a larger substantial mains powered one. Very good jigs are available to convert the tool into a pillar drill.

7 Orbital sander
A good aid to final finishing, but do not start with too coarse a grit – as the plate moves in an orbit rather than in a straight backwards and forwards motion, this machine can put marks into the timber. Use hand methods first and only use this machine with approximately 120 grit or finer. When you have a lot of sanding to do, however, it does relieve a lot of very hard work and the better models can produce very acceptable results.

8 Planer
The planer can remove a lot of the hard work from timber preparation, when it is best used held in the hands. It can also be inverted and fixed in a stand to act as a small surfacing planer. You can achieve a large measure of accuracy in this way but you must remember to follow the safety instructions very carefully.

9 Biscuit jointer
A fairly recent development which is largely used to substitute for dowels and tongues. It is a very effective machine for cutting the precise hole needed to accept the specially prepared biscuit inserts and it makes cabinet jointing very easy. It has the advantage that it can be used both on solid timber and on manmade board.

Spraying

Finishing can be completely carried out by hand methods, but there may be occasions when you wish to apply paint, stain, varnish or lacquer with a spray gun. Once you have mastered the technique, spraying gives a perfectly even finish. There are two main spraying methods: air spraying, where the finishing liquid is atomized with compressed air; and airless spraying, where the finish is compressed to atomize it and no compressed air is needed.

ENVIRONMENT

You need an area which can be separated from the working space, to prevent the mist that forms during spraying (overspray) from contaminating equipment and work in progress. An extractor fan is necessary to remove fumes and overspray, as is some form of non-inflammable curtaining or partition to separate the space. If much has to be done, you will probably need to invest in a specialized spray booth.

You will need to make some form of rotating platform upon which the work will stand and some form of racking or shelving so that finished work can dry or cure.

Safety

Most finishing materials are flammable and potentially explosive when sprayed as a fine mist in air. There must be no naked flames or lights. Do not smoke!

The fumes given off by spraying can be harmful and

Dust mask

Air-supplied mask

Air-supplied hood

Vapour mask

you will need some form of mask. The simplest is a dust mask, but for some finishes, a vapour mask can be necessary. With a lot of spraying you may need an air-supplied mask, or an air-supplied helmet or hood, both of which provide an independent air supply. ▲

Compressed air assisted spraying

An electrically-powered compressor delivers filtered air to a spray gun. The compressor consists of a pump or motor, a tank into which the air is delivered and stored (with a relief valve and a means of draining off surplus water), a condenser to clean and dry the air, and a regulator to provide constant airflow at a pre-set pressure. Several different types of spray gun may be used with compressed air. ▼

Regulator

Condenser filter

Pump

Motor

Tank

Safety valve

Water condensation drain

Vent hole

Syphon or suction spray gun

This finish reservoir is attached underneath the gun's grip. As the compressed air passes through the gun, suction draws liquid up and delivers it to the spray head. ▲

Gravity-fed spray gun

The finish is held in a small cup on top of the handset, and enters the gun by gravity. A useful gun for a home workshop. ▲

Airbrush

This can be used for very small jobs. It provides precise control and is only worth considering if you have a small, precise job to do and can borrow or hire one. ▼

Pressure-fed spray gun

The paint or lacquer is held in a pressurized container so the finish is delivered to the gun under pressure. It is convenient to use since there is little weight in the handset, but is limited to large-scale spraying operations rather than the home workshop. ▼

Airline

Air feed to gun

Air feed to lacquer container

Gun

Compressor

Lacquer

Lacquer feed to gun

Atomizing the finish

However the finish is delivered to the gun, it is at the nozzle that the material is changed from a fluid to a spray and there are two types of mixing cap to do this job.

Lacquer stream   Air stream

Atomized spray

Fluid control needle

External mixing cap

The liquid stream is ejected from the gun nozzle and the compressed air atomizes the liquid into a spray outside the nozzle. It gives accurate control of the spray pattern, since airflow can be adjusted, and is good for fast-drying lacquers. ▲

Compressed lacquer

Small orifice   Atomized spray

Internal mixing cap

Generally used with airless equipment, the liquid is pressurized inside the cap, the spray shape and pattern being determined by the shape of the nozzle orifice. ▲

Pattern control

Fluid control

Air valve

Trigger

Air feed from compressor

Air cap

Lacquer feed (pressure container or syphon cup)

Adjustment and cleaning

Controls on the handset adjust delivery rates of air and finish. The air flow adjuster controls the rate of air flow: high flow for thicker material, lower for thinner ones. This can sometimes be controlled at the compressor rather than at the gun. The pattern control regulates the quantity of air flowing to the mixing cap and this changes the spray pattern. The flow of material is controlled by adjusting the fluid control and amount of trigger movement. The procedure is – fill the lacquer container, spray and set the air flow adjuster, adjust the fluid control to obtain an even coat of finish, adjust the pattern control to give the required spread and shape and, finally, the pattern direction.

Clean the gun each time you use it by spraying lacquer thinners through the system. Occasionally take the gun apart and thoroughly clean and reassemble. ▲

Airless spraying

The principle of airless spraying is that the finish is pressurized and forced out of the spray orifice in an atomized form. This system is limited to large equipment for bulk or industrial use, but there are a few adaptations for smaller users. ▼

Pressurized container

Spray gun

Lacquer feed line

Electric spray gun

A small gun is available which follows the system described above, but on a scale suitable for home use. The results can be quite fair, but the disadvantage is that the finish has to be at a specific viscosity for it to be sprayed well. It must be thinned to a specific consistency using a viscosity cup. This is a measured container with a hole in the bottom, the contents of which must empty in a specific time. It is more useful for finishes that are near the correct viscosity, since over-thinning can affect some finishes. ▼

Internal mix cap

Electric motor

Pump

Trigger

Electric cable

Feed tube

Aerosol spray

Commonly available for automotive finishes, this can give good results but is an expensive way to buy paint. It may be difficult to find clear lacquer suitable for woodwork.

Glass jar aerosol

A glass jar, with aerosol top allows you to spray whatever finish you wish. It is necessary to use the fluid at the correct viscosity. ▼

FURTHER INFORMATION	
9	Safety first
60-61	Finishes
89	Using a spray gun

Nursery Furniture

This nursery furniture is an ideal opportunity to explore the possibilities of working manmade board using hand power tools. The construction is straightforward, the joints can be tongued and grooved using a router, or biscuit jointer. The decorative possibilities are limited only by your imagination.

AIMS OF THE PROJECT
To give experience in cutting, shaping and jointing manmade board.

TOOLS YOU WILL NEED
Coping saw, power jigsaw or bandsaw
Power router or biscuit jointer
Pencil
Rule
Marking gauge
Marking knife
Jack plane
Try square
Sash cramps
G-cramps
Sanding block

TIME TO ALLOW
Time lies in assembly since components are assembled in stages and the glue must cure before moving on to the next stage.
It could well take a couple of weekends to do the machining and jointing, and a couple of weeks of work in the evenings jointing components.

REMEMBER
Any manmade board needs one or more coats of sealer before applying the finishing colour coat. Use sanding sealer or a primer/filler. Sealing and finishing coats can be brushed on, but if you wish, use this project to learn how to use a spraygun.

HEALTH AND SAFETY
Follow the safe working procedures outlined on page 9.

CHOOSING MATERIAL
MDF has been used here because it is so simple to finish, ply or chipboard would do equally well.

With this project, the "cutting list" is in the form of a drawn layout, rather than a set of components so that you can reduce waste (see overleaf).

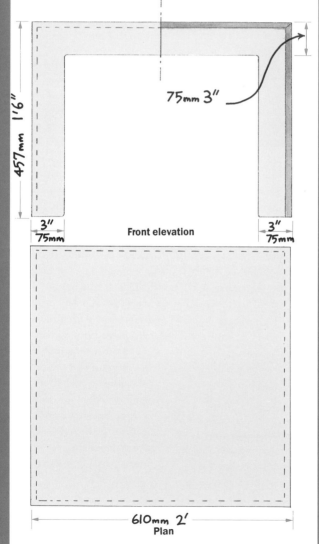

75mm 3"

457mm 1'6"

3" 75mm

Front elevation

3" 75mm

610mm 2'
Plan

280mm 11"

130mm 5"

20mm 3/4"

265mm 10½"

190mm 7½"

Centro lino

Front elevation

305mm 12"

75mm 3"

50mm 2"

150mm 6"

25mm 1"

432mm 15"

245mm 9¾"

Sectional side elevation
through centre line

45mm 1¼"

50mm
2"

Plan

Exploded diagram

PLANS

The drawings on this page
show the elevations and
sections, together with an
exploded perspective view
of the finished piece.

Scale 1:9

Exploded diagram

The legs are grouped
2 around the table top. You
will need either a coping saw
or a power jigsaw to cut the
'L'-shaped pieces for the
legs. Clean up any rough
edges with a sanding block.

JOINTING THE LEGS

3 The 8 "L"-shaped pieces
are mitred together in
pairs to form four leg-and-rail
corner components. To fit
these to the top you can
either mitre the top and the
tops of the corner
components, or set the legs
directly under the top. The
project is described using
mitres all round.

MAKING THE TABLE

1 Follow the diagram to
mark out components on
the board. The board is cut in
order to utilize the material
as economically as
possible. ▼

CUTTING MITRES

4 Plane a 45 degree mitre
all round the table top,
and also around the outer
edges of the eight "L"-shaped
leg components.
Alternatively, cut the mitres
using a router. ▲

MAKING THE JOINTS

5 Set the router with
a small cutter (4.5mm/
$^{3}/_{16}$in) and cut grooves for the
tongues along the mitred
surfaces. You will need to cut
tongues from a piece of ply of
the same thickness as the
grooves. ▼

Alternatively, use a
6 biscuit jointer to make
short grooves for biscuits.

Assemble the four
7 corner joints using two
"L-"shaped pieces per corner.
Note that the long lengths
form the legs and the short
lengths fit to the top. Use
masking tape to hold the
joints together. Ensure that
the corners are square and
let the glue cure before
working on them further. ▼

8 Take two leg assemblies and glue them to the top on opposite corners. The geometry of the joint should mean that everything will come square when these joints are glued and cramped home. Again, let the adhesive cure before going on to the next stage. ▲

9 With the first legs in position, fit the final pair. Not only will you be jointing legs to top, but you will be jointing the rail between each leg section. Glue these last two leg components in position and when the glue has cured your table structure should be finished and very strong.

10 The corners of the table are very sharp, however, and you will need to plane the outside corners. For small children a larger rounded edge may be preferable and this is a chance to use the router with a rounding-over or other specially-shaped cutter.

11 Now sand the table all over in preparation for the sealing coat. MDF needs slightly less sealing than either chipboard or ply but any manmade board needs one or more sealing coats before applying the finished colour coat. Sand down between each coat. ▼

12 Apply the finishing coat or coats in the colour you have chosen. Next apply any decorative effects you have. This project used "falling letters", but you will no doubt think of a variety of ways of adding interest.

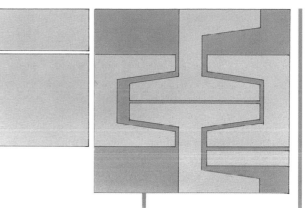

CHAIR

13 Mark out components on the board as shown in the diagram. Two thicknesses of board are specified: 10mm (3/8in) for the main chair frame and 3mm (1/8in) or 4.5mm (3/16in) for the seat and back. If you are making more than one chair you will probably be able to use the material more economically. ▲

14 Cut the components from the board, using a jigsaw.

FURTHER INFORMATION	
47	Preparing the surface
76-77	Power hand tools
86-87	Using a router

15 Plane all components to the required shape. It is easiest to work all the edges square at this stage. Pay attention to the sloping angle on the inside edges of the legs. ▲

16 Work the mitres on the four corners of the main sections. Stop the mitre on the back leg above the seat at the position shown and also at the top corner where the top rail fits.

17 Cut rebates for the seat and the back rest. ▲

18 Make tongues and grooves or biscuit joints.

19 Assemble the frame dry, adjust, and check. If all is well glue the frame, the two sides, the back and front and the top rail and let the glue cure. ▶

20 If you have used thin material for the seat and back it will bend to the curve easily. When making the prototype 6mm (¼in) MDF was used and the seat and back shapes had to be pre-curved before fitting. If you need to do this, cramp the pieces in a rough jig, having cut the seat and back very slightly over-size. ▼

21 You will then need to fit the seat in position and it is a tricky piece of measuring to get it to fit precisely. The seat fits in the rebates on all four sides except at the rear where it is cut away to fit inside the side frames. ▼

22 When the seat fits dry, glue and cramp in position. ▼

23 The same, but slightly easier procedure, applies for the back rest. Fit and glue in position. ▲

24 Now, as with the table, sand off sharp edges or use a router with a rounding-over cutter. ▲

25 Finish the chair using the same procedures that were used for the table. Use filler if necessary, sand all over, apply sealing coats and the finishing coat. ▲

26 The finished table and chair decorated with "falling letters". ▼

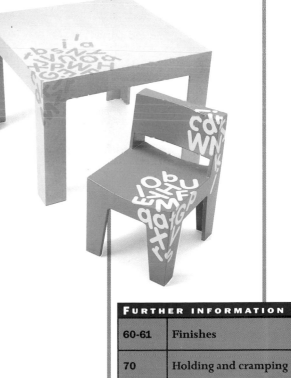

Using a Router

The router is a useful tool and has become popular with woodworkers because it can do so many jobs that were once the province of specialized tools such as rebate planes, plough planes and moulding planes.

FITTING CUTTERS

1 Use a spanner to tighten the collet so that it grips the cutter firmly. Some machines have a spindle lock, others need a pin through the spindle to immobilize it while you tighten the collet nut. ▼

2 If your router does not have a collet nut, use two spanners, one to grip the spindle and one to tighten the collet nut. Arrange the spanners in a V-formation so that you can squeeze them in one hand. ▼

USING A ROUTER

1 To prevent the wood burning and to lengthen the life of your cutters, take a series of shallow cuts, rather than attempting to make one deep cut. As a general rule, only cut to a depth equal to half the cutter diameter with any one cut. ▲

2 Most routers are of the plunge type, and you can set the depth of cut in advance, using the depth stop. Some routers have rotating multi-depth stops so that you can set the range of cuts for the job. The router illustrated has three threaded stops in a revolving holder to give a sequence of cutting depths. ▲

3 Router cutters rotate in a clockwise direction, so as the machine is pushed forward it has a tendency to pull to the left. In cutting a groove with the fence on the right-hand side the router's leftward pull holds the fence firmly against the work. ▼

4 To operate the plunging router, ensure that the cutter is locked in a raised position above the work. Position the router where you want to begin the cut. Switch on the router. ▼

5 Loosen the plunge handle to plunge the cutter into the timber as far as the depth stop. Move the router forward to make the cut. Keep the router moving steadily. Moving too fast may overload the motor, too slow may burn the work and damage the cutter. With experience, the sound of the motor is your best guide. ▲

6 At the end of the cut, loosen the plunge handle and let the cutter retract from the work. Then switch off. This is the basic freehand process. ▲

ROUTING GROOVES

1 To cut a groove parallel to the edge of the wood, use the straight fence supplied with the router. Mark the position of the groove on the wood and adjust the fence so that the cutter runs parallel to the edge. For a deeper cut, make a series of passes. ▶

2 Use a batten as a guide to cut a groove on a wide board, or a groove that is not parallel to an edge. Mark the groove position, measure from the cutter to the edge of the router base, and clamp the batten this distance from the groove. Run the router against the batten. ▶

3 To cut a wide groove in the middle of a board, use two battens. Position each one so it allows the router to cut the sides of the groove, then rout out the centre. ▶

ROUTING REBATES, CHAMFERS AND PROFILES ON EDGES

1 Moulding and edging cutters have a guide pin or a ballbearing guide which runs along the edge of the wood below the rotating cutter blades so that the cutter can be used without a guide fence. ▼

2 If the work is straight and not too wide, shape the edge by running the guide fence along the opposite side. ▼

3 To cut shapes and edges, use a template and a guide bush. The guide bush is screwed into the router base. It allows the router to follow the edge of a template. The size of the guide bush relates to the cutter diameter. There should be a 2 to 3mm (⅛in) gap between the cutter and the guide. ▲

4 Make the template from MDF or plywood. Roughly cut the workpiece oversize and secure the template to it with double-sided tape. Run the guide bush along the edge of the template, taking a series of cuts, if necessary, to shape the edge of the work. ▼

FURTHER INFORMATION	
9	Safety first
76-77	Power hand tools

Biscuit Jointing

The biscuit jointer is a power tool that has been developed to make an alternative to traditional edge and butt joints such as tongue and groove or dowel joints. The closest traditional equivalent is the loose tongue joint.

The biscuit jointer offers a simple, quick and accurate way of making such joints in either timber or man-made boards. It is widely used in small-scale industrial workshops.

A biscuit joint is not as strong as mortise and tenon or dovetail joints and should not be used on the corners of frames.

The biscuit jointer itself is a small-diameter circular saw held safely in the body of the machine. The blade is plunged into the wood to make a groove for the biscuit in one cut.

The baseplate and guide fence enable the machine to be positioned accurately for the cut. There is also a bevel fence for cutting biscuit grooves in mitre joints.

An insert made of compressed beech, shaped like a lozenge, a leaf or a biscuit is inserted into the groove.

USING A BISCUIT JOINTER

1 First cut precise butt joints, either by saw or plane. Check both faces with a square to ensure they are at 90 degrees along their whole length. ▲

2 Mark the centres of the biscuits on both boards. Biscuits can be spaced with 50 to 75mm (2 to 3in) left between each biscuit. ▲

3 Set the jointer to make its cut in the centre of the board's thickness. Holding the machine in position, switch it on and carefully make a plunge cut. Withdraw the blade without disturbing the position of the machine. ▶

"L" Joints

4 For "L" joints leave the fence in position, and align the machine at the end of the second board. Make the cut. ▶

"T" Joints

5 For "T" joints cut grooves in the panel end as described in (step 3) above. To cut the grooves in the second board, remove the guide fence, clamp a board or batten on the work and align the machine against this to make the cut. ▶

Using a Spray Gun

Joining mitres

6 To join mitres set the jointer to make its cut near the inside corner of the mitre for greater strength. ▼

7 One method is to set the guide fence against the edge of the board to make the cut. ▼

8 Alternatively, clamp the mitred panel securely onto another panel and rest the machine's bevel against the second panel to make the cut. ▲

Assembly

9 To assemble the joint use a thin wooden spatula to make sure glue goes right into the grooves. Glue the panels first, then fit the biscuits dry, and assemble. The biscuits swell when wet and grip in the grooves to add strength. Cramp the joint. ▲

Spraying should be done in a large, dust-free, well-ventilated room and in a good light. If you are spraying outdoors, choose a still, dry day.

Cover everything else in the vicinity with newspaper or plastic sheet. For your own safety, wear a mask covering your nose and mouth.

SPRAYING PRACTICE

1 Before spraying, stir thoroughly with a stick, remove the stick and hold it at a 45° angle. The liquid is the correct consistency when it runs off in a steady stream. ▲

2 Practice first on scrap wood, experimenting with spray adjustment and distance from the work. Spray in smooth, steady strokes, keeping the spray at right angles to the work. ▲

3 Do not spray in an arc, this results in uneven coating, and do not jerk the gun. Move the gun at a consistent speed so the thickness of the finish remains constant. ▲

4 Overlap the strokes by about 50 per cent, and spray past the ends of the work. Start moving the gun before you pull the trigger and release the trigger before stopping the gun at the end of a stroke. ▲

FURTHER INFORMATION	
9	Safety first
60-61	Finishes
76-77	Power hand tools
78-79	Spraying

MDF and Colour

Manmade boards are immensely versatile to use to create simple furniture. With power and machine tools they can be quickly cut to shape and joined to make furniture for children from babies to teenagers.

The basic techniques of working MDF and other manmade board can be applied to making a whole range of nursery furniture including cupboards and desks as well as the table and chairs.

Manmade boards also take paint and other decorative finishes so well that a wide range of decorative ideas can be applied, from variations in colour and texture, to complete fairytale scenes.

The whole approach to working with manmade board is different from solid wood since the problem of timber movement does not exist. This gives the opportunity to design and construct forms that can only be successfully made in these materials. To investigate possible structures in manmade board, make scale models from cardboard as well as sketches.

GETTING STARTED

Once you have mastered the basic jointing and finishing techniques, the only limit is your imagination. Children's furniture provides the ideal opportunity to exploit the versatility of manmade board.

ROBERT VENTURI ●
Coloured chair
Manufactured boards can be shaped and jointed successfully in ways that just would not work with solid timber. The symmetrical back and colouring give this chair a lively look, while its splayed legs make it sturdy and stable. ▲

ROBERT VENTURI ● *Table*
Each of the legs faces in a different direction, giving the table the same lively feel as the chair. Spattered and sponged paint needs little artistic ability, but is a very effective way of working with colours. ◄

JOHN ANDERSON ● *Sea chest*
An opportunity to use laminating techniques to make the waves. The full sails and waving flags are detailed touches that add to the jaunty appearance. The paint effects, though simple, are also applied with attention to detail. ▶

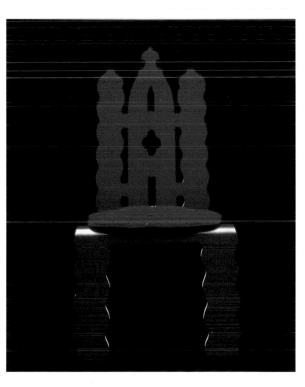

JAKKI DEHN ● *Child's cot*
The chest of drawers base is practical and gives stability, large industrial castors are added for mobility. The paint effect — a simple pattern on alternate stripes — can be adapted to any colour scheme. Note "tail" for suspending a mobile. ▲

ROBERT VENTURI ● *Chair*
Seat and front legs are cut from one piece and bent at right angles, making a smooth curve. The glossy finish enhances the bright paint. ◀

FURTHER INFORMATION	
80-85	Module 3: nursery furniture

Machine Tools

Powerful modern machinery enables you to do precise work at speed and on a scale that few home woodworkers would have attempted when only hand tools were available. Always treat machines with a great deal of respect and never use a machine when you are tired or affected by drugs or alcohol. Also never be tempted to do a job on your own when you really need someone else to support the work, for safety. If you do not take risks, these tools will save you much time and be a pleasure to use.

Fretsaw

The fretsaw can make very fine internal cuts on a complex shape making it a fairly specialized machine associated with model-making more often than furnituremaking. However, good quality machines will cut quite thick timber and there is a large range of blades to choose from. A very fine cut can be achieved needing little or no subsequent work. ▲

Radial arm saw

Not only sawing, but grooving, rebating and shaping can be achieved with this saw. The blade can be rotated and angled in many directions to allow mitres and bevels to be cut. A wide range of blades is available and moulding heads can also be fitted. Some woodworkers are devotees of this machine, others are not entirely convinced of the safety aspects of some operations. ▶

Saw blades

Saw blades are designed for a variety of jobs, from ripping to crosscutting, some also give a very smooth finish. It is always worth buying blades with tungsten carbide tips. They are more expensive and need to be professionally sharpened but they stay sharp much longer. ▲

Table saw

The table or dimension saw allows you to rip and crosscut with speed and accuracy. The blade can be raised, lowered and tilted to cut bevels. It will also cut grooves and rebates.

However it is essential for the blade to be properly guarded at all times. If you remove the top guard for any operations ensure you take greatest care. ▼

Bandsaw

Both straight cuts, curves and thick timber can be cut on this useful general purpose machine. The blade is a fast-cutting continuous strip running over two or three wheels, its downward thrust means there is no danger of kickback. The bandsaw takes up little floor space and the thin blade means little timber is wasted in the kerf. ▶

Planer thicknesser

This is the second machine to buy after the table saw. The saw converts material. The planer thicknesser prepares it. For small workshops the combination machine is excellent and some good models are available. As with hand planes, the longer the table (or plane), the flatter and straighter the results. Most small machines have short tables and when using them check that you are achieving straight and flat work. After facing and edging timber with the planer, the thicknesser will size it to width and thickness. ▲

Disc and belt sander

Generally this machine is most useful for small-scale pieces, but be very careful since it can easily remove too much. You need a precise approach for good results. You can adjust the fence and the table on the disc sander for accurate smoothing of angles and end grain. ▶

Pillar drill

This is the big brother of the power hand drill. Some woodworkers prefer a machine especially for mortises which can also drill, but a drill which can take a mortising attachment is preferable. The pillar drill generally has a wide range of speeds and is either floor or bench mounted with an adjustable table which can be raised or lowered. Floor-mounted machines allow you to drill long items. ▶

Hollow chisel mortiser

If your work develops so you have lots of mortises to make, this is a useful investment. The auger bit in the centre cuts the hole and the square sharp chisel is pressed into the wood to make a clean cut. Most home workshop models take square chisels 6mm to 20mm (¼in to ¾in) wide. ▲

Universal/combination machines

These machines generally include a table saw, spindle moulder, overhead planer, thicknesser, mortiser and sometimes a lathe.

At first sight these seem an attractive proposition, however the universal machine is limited and you cannot upgrade freely.

FURTHER INFORMATION	
9	Safety first
54-55	Workshop planning
76-77	Power hand tools

Principles of Drawer Making

Drawers are boxes with an open top, designed to slide into a box with an open front, a cabinet. Drawers can be in a huge range of sizes and shapes, either to store and aid retrieval of specific objects or to fit in with the proportions and details of a particular piece of furniture. Most drawers do both these tasks. These two pages look at how the drawer has traditionally been made and at alternative methods.

Cross rail

TRADITIONAL DRAWER CONSTRUCTION

The components of a drawer consist of the front, two sides, back and bottom. The lap dovetails joining the sides and front tighten as the drawer is pulled out and so use the dovetails to contribute to the construction and strength of the drawer. The back is through dovetailed to the sides.

The parts of a drawer, constructed using traditional methods.

Wide drawers

Wide drawers often need the support of a central rail on the bottom, called a muntin. It is fitted with a tenon into the front and a notch at the back. The drawer bottom is made in two parts, each sliding into grooves in the side and the muntin. ▼

Drawer stops

A drawer should never be the full depth of a cabinet, if it fits flush between the sides and the cross rails a drawer stop is needed. The easiest way is to screw or pin a block in place. The finer way is to let an L-shaped block into a small mortise in the cross rail. ▲

Fitting a drawer bottom

The bottom slides in grooves on the sides to a groove in the front. The back is cut high to allow the bottom panel to slide in underneath it. ▼

If a thicker drawer bottom, or one made of solid wood, is required, then this can be accommodated by chamfering the bottom around the edges. ▼

Sometimes with fine, thin, drawer sides, there is not enough timber to cut a groove, so drawer slips are applied. These can be shaped, with a half round inside the drawer. ▼

At the front the slip has a tenon cut to fit into the front groove, and at the rear it is notched to fit under the back. ▼

The bottom is screwed at the back only, in a slot to allow for movement. ▼

Conventional drawer bottom

Chamfered drawer bottom

Applied half round drawer slips

The bottom tongued into grooved slips

Front

Back

Fitting a drawer front

There are various ways in which a drawer front can be fitted into a cabinet. It can fit flush between the cross rails. An alternative flush-fitting method uses a small section of wood called a "cock bead" let into the four front edges of the drawer front. This gives an interesting visual detail, but also makes the drawer slightly easier to fit than the previous method. Fronts can sit in front of cross rails and this method has been used in the projects. Fronts can project above or below the cross rail. ▼

Short cuts in drawer making

A false front can be screwed onto a simple drawer. Use this method where the drawers cover the front of a cabinet, or to match the grain pattern in a series of fronts.

Other joints used to make drawers include the comb or finger joint which is quick to cut by machine and often used in commercial drawer making. A simple lap joint relies on the strength of the glue, avoid this unless the work is less than final. Mitre joints strengthened with either tongues or biscuits may also be used.

Dovetail housings can join the sides to the front. Either a complete or barefaced housing will tighten up as the drawer is pulled out in the same way as through or lapped dovetails.

A tray is a drawer with low sides. These can often be made with a simple frame, applying the bottom, flush or in a rebate, with glue and pins or screws. It is possible to find commercially-produced drawers, either in plastic, injection moulded, or in the form of wire baskets. These items work well in kitchen fittings. ▼

DRAWER RUNNERS

The traditional way is to fit drawer runners into stopped housings in the cabinet sides. Runners are stub tenoned into the front cross rails, and no glue is used. Another common method is to make a stopped groove on the drawer sides, cut a batten to fit the groove, and then glue and screw the batten to the cabinet sides.

Runners glued and screwed to the cabinet

To fit a drawer under a surface or shelf, screw battens to the drawer sides to run on battens screwed to the underside of the shelf.

A drawer suspended beneath a surface

Flush fitting drawer front

Cock beaded drawer front

Projecting drawer front

Front projects above or below the cross rails

Comb or finger joint

Lap joint

Mitre with tongue

Mitre with biscuits

Dovetail housing

A tray, a simple frame with bottom pinned or screwed in place.

FURTHER INFORMATION	
58-59	Principles of cabinet construction
68-69	Making dovetail joints
96-105	Module 4: chest of drawers
124-129	Module 6: desk

Chest of Drawers

The next stage in cabinet construction after making the simple wall-hung cabinet is the making and fitting of drawers.

This cabinet contains four drawers, each of a different depth. The drawers are opened by finger grooves positioned so that they form a distinctive design feature across the cabinet front.

Classic fine furniture-making techniques used in this chest of drawers include dovetail drawer joints, and dustboards between the drawers.

AIMS OF THE PROJECT
To give practice and build competence in making a set of drawers to fit into a cabinet.

TOOLS YOU WILL NEED
Chalk
Pencil
Rule
Panel saw
Marking gauge
Marking knife
Jack plane
Dovetail saw
Range of chisels for dovetails
Mortise gauge
Mortise chisel
Try square
Power router
Biscuit jointer or drill depending on your choice of corner joints
Sash cramps
Cabinet scraper
Sanding block

TIME TO ALLOW
Depending upon the joints you use, the cabinet should only take two or three weekends' work. However the new skill of making drawers will take more time to acquire.

REMEMBER
Treat this project in stages. First the carcase, second the interior fittings and drawer runners and, third, the drawers. Precise working is essential. The carcase must be square and the spaces for the drawers parallel.

HEALTH AND SAFETY
Follow the safe working procedures outlined on page 9.

CHOOSING WOOD

If you have made the other projects in order, you will now have experience in using both solid wood and manmade board.

The prototype was made from ash. For this first project making drawers, choose a wood that is fairly easy to work. Beech is useful for the drawer sides and interior fitting of the cabinet, while the drawer fronts and outside of the cabinet can be any wood of your choice.

No	Sawn	Planed
CUTTING LIST: BODY		
2	SIDES 686mm x 343mm x 30mm 2ft 3in x 1ft 1½in x 1¼in	660mm x 330mm x 25mm 2ft 2in x 1ft 1in x 1in
1	TOP 432mm x 343mm x 30mm 1ft 5in x 1ft 1½in x 1¼in	406mm x 330mm x 25mm 1ft 4in x 1ft 1in x 1in
1	BOTTOM RAIL 432mm x 75mm x 25mm 1ft 5in x 3in x 1in	406mm x 72mm x 20mm 1ft 4in x 2⅞in x ¾in
8	DRAWER CROSS RAILS 406mm x 57mm x 20mm 1ft 4in x 2¼in x ¾in	50mm x 12mm 2in x ½in
8	DRAWER RUNNERS 200mm x 38mm x 20mm 8in x 1½in x ¾in	30mm x 12mm 1¼in x ½in
1	CABINET BACK 660mm x 406mm x 6mm plywood 2ft 2in x 1ft 4in x ¼in	
4	DUST BOARDS 330mm x 200mm x 6mm plywood 1ft 1in x 8in x ¼in	
+ adhesive, finishing, screws		

CUTTING LIST: DRAWERS

No	Sawn	Planed
	DRAWER No 1 (TOP)	
1	FRONT 380mm x 105 x 25mm 1ft 3in x 4¼in x 1in	356mm x 100mm x 20mm 1ft 2in x 4in x ¾in
2	SIDES 305mm x 90mm x 20mm 12in x 3¾in x ¾in	280mm x 85mm x 12mm 11in x 3½in x ½in
1	BACK 380mm x 75mm x 20mm 1ft 3in x 3in x ¾in	356mm x 72mm x 10mm 1ft 2in x 2⅞in x ⅜in
1	BOTTOM 356mm x 280mm x 6mm plywood 1ft 2in x 11in x ¼in	

The cutting list for the other 3 drawers is similar to drawer 1, but some parts change in width since the drawer depth increases. The widths are:

Sawn	Planed
2nd DRAWER Front 140mm (5½in) Sides 120mm (4¾in) Back 100mm (4in)	130mm (5in) 115mm (4½in) 95mm (3⅞in)
3rd DRAWER Front 162mm (6½in) Sides 146mm (5¾in) Back 130mm (5in)	150mm (6in) 140mm (5½in) 122mm (4⅞in)
4th DRAWER (BOTTOM) Front 190mm (7½in) Sides 172mm (6¾in) Back 150mm (6in)	180mm (7in) 162mm (6½in) 148mm (5⅞in)
+ adhesive, finishing, screws	

PLANS

The drawings on this page and overleaf show the elevations and sections, together with an exploded perspective view of the finished piece.

Scale 1:8

660mm 2'2"

406mm 1'4"

Centre line

Centre line

Sectional half plan (drawers removed)

330mm 1'1"

25mm 1"

100mm 4"

130mm 5"

150mm 6"

180mm 7"

75mm 3"

50mm 2"

234mm 9⅛"

50mm 2"

12mm ½"

20mm ¾"

Sectional side elevation through centre line

FURTHER INFORMATION	
30-31	Reading drawings
58-59	Principles of cabinet construction
94-95	Principles of drawer making

9mm 3/8"   6mm 1/4"

25mm 1"

100mm 4"

**Section showing detail of
cabinet and top drawers**

Scale ½ size

Joints at junction of top and
sides can be dovetailed as
shown in this drawing or
mitred with tongues or biscuits
as shown in the photographs

Drawer runners

Dust board

Cross rails

Bottom cross rails

Exploded diagram

TIMBER PURCHASE

1 The top and sides are made from 30mm (1¼in) timber, whereas most of the rest will come from 25mm or 20mm (1in or ¾in) timber. The back is made of plywood. Dustboards between the drawers are also made of ply and the drawers have ply bottoms.

2 Mark and cut out all components. Plane face side, face edge, width and thickness, leaving slightly over length.

CARCASE CONSTRUCTION

3 Mark out the two sides and the top. The carcase consists of the sides and top, a bottom cross rail and a back panel.

4 Make the corner joints. The wall-hung cabinet project used secret mitre dovetail corner joints. Continue to practise by making dovetails on the top two corners or, mitre these joints and use tongues, biscuits or dowels. This is an ideal project to use tongues if you have a router.

5 It is essential to get a very good mitre at these two corners. You will probably spend some time planing the mitre and ensuring that it is a good fit at 90°.

6 Rout the groove in the mitre for the tongues, or use a biscuit jointer. ▼

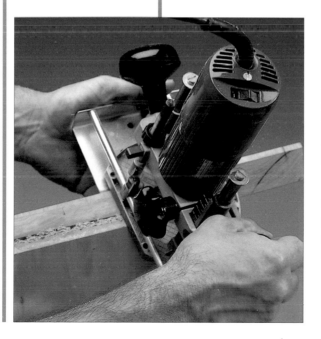

7 Place the tongue in the groove and fit the joint dry. ▶

8 Mark the bottom rail and make the joints that will hold it in place. The rail has a stub tenon fitted into mortises on the two sides. ▲

FURTHER INFORMATION	
32-33	Basic jointing
44-45	Making a mortise and tenon joint
68-69	Making dovetail joints

9 Work the groove for the back panel in the top and the sides. ▲

10 Cut and fit the ply back. Its function is to hold the cabinet square and, as is normal practice, it slides into place from the bottom and will later be fixed to one of the cross rails.

11 Sand the interior, then apply a finish if required (see **23**).

DRAWER RUNNERS AND CROSS RAILS

12 Under each drawer is a frame consisting of a runner at each side and a front and back cross rail. A ply dustboard is set within grooves cut on the inside faces of these pieces.

13 The front and back cross rails are glued in place. The runners and dust boards are slightly undersize from front to back. The runners are tenoned into the groove in the cross rails.

14 The design assumes that the sides are made from solid wood, therefore there is likely to be timber movement. To allow for expansion and contraction, the tenon on the runners is fitted tight and glued at the front, while at the back the tenon and its shoulder are cut short about 3mm (⅛in) to allow for any back to front movement in the cabinet.

16 Make stub tenons in the back and front cross rails and make corresponding mortises on the inside of the cabinet. Ensure that these shoulders are the same as those on the bottom cabinet rail. ▼

17 In order to fit the dustboard, work the groove on the inside edges of the cross rails as shown in the drawing.

18 Fit the carcase together dry. Make any adjustments If necessary and take it apart again. ▶

19 Mark the positions of the front to back drawer runners on the inside of the sides. These are tenoned not into a mortise, but into the groove in the cross rails. ▶

20 Run a groove for the dustboard in each runner.

21 Mark, cut and fit four plywood dust boards.

22 Try assembling these components together. If all is well, check that all these Internal components are sanded and you can glue the carcase together. ▼

FURTHER INFORMATION	
70	Holding and cramping
86-87	Using a router

25 Each drawer back is not a tight fit vertically since it sits on the drawer bottom and does not extend the full depth of the drawer. It does, however, need to fit precisely across the carcase and you should be able to insert it from front to back. ▶

23 It is not usual to finish inside a cabinet where drawers are fitted, but you can apply a simple sealing coat of the chosen finish if you wish. Drawers should slide wood on to wood. You should now have a firm carcase structure in which to run the drawers. ▲

MAKING DRAWERS

24 Make and fit one drawer at a time, repeating the procedure for the other three. Plane the drawer sides so that they are an exact fit and slide in and out of the carcase. ▶

26 Take the drawer front and fit it into its opening. It should fit exactly on the inside face from end to end, but make a bevel so that it tapers towards the outside face which is slightly longer. ▶

27 You will see from the drawing that the top drawer fits from the underside of the cabinet top to the lower face of the first drawer rail. ▶

28 Once sides, back and front have been fitted, make the groove for the drawer bottom on the inside of the two sides and the front.

29 Mark the dovetail joints. Lap dovetails join the front to the sides. ▲

FURTHER INFORMATION	
71	Finishing
68-69	Making dovetail joints
94-95	Principles of drawer making

30 Through dovetails join the sides to the back. ▲

31 Remember to make allowances for the handle groove that is on the lower edge of the top drawer. The groove is on the upper edge of the second drawer, the lower edge of the third drawer and the upper edge of the bottom drawer. When assembled the grooves make a decorative feature, running across the cabinet.

32 Cut the dovetails with care. Make sure that your gauge lines are precisely the thickness of the components. This technique does not allow for major planing of the drawer sides to ensure fit. The precise marking of the drawer back and front should ensure the drawer fits if the dovetails have been well made, with only a slight cleaning up necessary.

33 Mark the ply bottom and cut to fit. ▲

34 Slide the bottom into place. The drawer bottom is not glued in the grooves, slot it in place and insert two screws at the back, through the drawer bottom up into the drawer back. Assemble the drawer dry and check that it is a tight fit. ▲

35 Add glue and assemble the drawer. When the glue has cured it should only need a few touches of the plane to enable the drawer to run smoothly in its space. ▼

36 Now you have mastered drawer making on the first one, follow the same procedure for the other three.

37 The cabinet back is fitted with a couple of screws through the back into the bottom back drawer rail.

38 Sand the carcase and the drawer fronts and apply the final finish.

39 The finished chest of drawers, waxed and polished – an asset to any room. ▲

Chest of Drawers

A cabinet to hold a range of drawers can be made almost any size or proportion, and the number and arrangement of drawers within it can also be varied in many ways. Make a scale drawing before embarking on any project.

Bear in mind what the drawers will be expected to hold and ensure they are not too large so that there is a danger of overloading them.

It is usual to have drawers lighter at the top, deepening to give a heavier more solid appearance towards the bottom. Many modern designers dispense with this rule to make interesting patterned arrangements of the drawer fronts.

HANK WOLLER ● *Skyscraper cabinet*
This piece contains lots of interest, using natural wood and colour for an effect which is enlivened by the textures and patterns of doors, drawers and cupboards. ▶

DRAWERS AND OPENINGS

Drawers can be combined with cupboard doors, or arranged in an asymmetrical pattern.

Drawer runners

Drawers can be bottom-run, as in the chest of drawers in Module 4, or side-run. Side-run drawers have a stopped groove routed out of the sides. This fits on a hardwood batten screwed and glued to the cabinet sides.

Ready-made drawer slide systems are available in a variety of designs to suit anything from small lightweight drawers to deep, heavy kitchen drawers. If you use these, the drawer front must overlap the cabinet to cover the space needed for the slide system.

Tall narrow cabinet.

Combination of wide and narrow drawers.

Symmetrical combination.

A modern, asymmetrical style.

HANDLES

As well as contributing to the appearance of the chest of drawers, handles must be easy to grasp and must be able to take the pull of a fully-loaded drawer. You can make handles yourself, either as an integral part of the drawer front, or to attach, or you can choose from an almost infinite range of bought handles.

Handle position

In classic furnituremaking, attached handles are never positioned on the centre line of the drawer or door, but just above it. This applies whether the handle is placed to the edge, as on a cupboard door, or in the centre. ▼

Handle position on a cupboard.

Handle position on a drawer.

Handle size

It is an important part of the design process to consider the size of handles and their relationship to the size of the drawer fronts. ▼

Consider handle size in proportion to drawer size.

Large handles will dominate the design.

Tiny handles can make an interesting detail feature.

Style of handles

Handles can be routed or carved out of the solid wood of the drawer front. They can be a subtle addition to the design, or they can play a more dominant part in the design.

Handles made from dowel section make a bold modern addition to the drawers. ▲

Rout out a recess for the handle in the drawer front. Insert a dowel section or carved peg. ▲

A bought handle set at an angle adds an unusual touch. ▲

An overhanging lip can be cut from the solid wood of the drawer front, or attached to the top of the drawer front. ▼

A grooved handle should be large enough for you to hook your fingers into. ▼

ROBERT INGHAM • *Chest of drawers*
This chest of drawers is an exquisite piece of furniture in its design, choice of material, detailing and making. ◀

Chairs and Their Construction

The chair has always been a great challenge to designers, this is why there are so many variations on such a common object.

Chairmaking developed into a specialized craft from the simple frame systems. Mortise and tenon joints are still widely used in chair making, and much use is also made of dowels.

The chair became the most shaped and carved area of the furnituremaker's craft. An important element in chair design has been the development of upholstery. Designers, particularly in this century, have evolved many different ideas for the chair, both complex and simple forms and, in some, very advanced structures. The chair can often be furniture as art. Its styles often echo major movements in art, architecture and design.

The back legs inserted at an angle

Traditional chairs: Windsor chairs

These were traditional chairs made in the beechwoods in Europe where good timber was available. The design shown is quite a refined version. Country furniture also evolved the type of chair with turned legs and rails, often with a rush seat. ▼

CHAIR CONSTRUCTION

While shaping has characterized the development of the chair, there are two common forms of normal chair construction: either make the two sides and join them together; or make the front and back and join these. The former generally happens with a complex arm and side shape, whilst the latter will generally be used when there is a complex back together with carved front legs.

Join the sides together

Join front to back

The 'D' frame

As chairs developed shape the old frame methods of construction were less appropriate and the chair maker developed the 'D' frame. The insertion of the back legs at an angle naturally gives a tapered back.

With the use of a steel band cramp and dowel joints between back and side rails and the back legs, the structure is glued into a very strong frame. It enabled shapely chairs to be produced before the development of laminating or formed plastic shells. ▶

Band cramp and dowel joints

Victorian

Windsor chair

Traditional chairs: bentwood chairs

In a sense following the Windsor tradition, the firm of Thonet developed bentwood designs in Austria and they produced a vast range of different forms. The one shown in the illustration is one of the timeless classics, the café chair. It was one of the first items of mass production, 4 million being shipped in component (knock down) parts into America during the last decade of the 19th century. It has often been copied, but never equalled. ▼

Bentwood café chair

Modern chairs

Since the late 19th century modern materials and manufacturing techniques have been fully exploited in chair design and manufacture.

After traditional Windsor and bentwood chairs, laminated forms were introduced and then later on metals and plastics became widely used. These developments are often found more widely in the contract market rather than in domestic furniture. ▶

Laminated chair by Alvar Aalto

Steel wire chair by E. Race

Moulded one-piece plastic chair by Verner Panton

During the periods of Art Nouveau and Art Deco, chairs became highly shaped and

SPECIAL APPROACHES

There are many specialized chairs for specialized uses, two common ones are folding chairs and stacking chairs.

Folding chairs

A very traditional folding wooden chair folds from front to back. The other method is to fold side to side. The chair by the Danish designer, Mogens Koch, is a lovely example of considered design.

Folding wooden chair

Folding wood and canvas chair

Stacking chairs

Stacking chairs are generally made of metal or plastic but the one shown here by Peter Danko uses laminated timber.

Stacking chair of laminated timber

decorated. The illustration shows a chair designed around the beginning of this century by the Catalan architect, Antoni Gaudi, of Barcelona, exemplifying the sculptural approach to the chairmaker's art. ▼

Art Nouveau chair designed by Antoni Gaudi

Moulded plywood chair designed by Charles Eames

In the mid 1950's Charles Eames designed the chair with a moulded ply seat and back – a design which combines simplicity with good posture and comfort. ▲

Upright Chair

Traditional chairmaking demands a high level of skill. The main challenge is that in order to fit the curves and angles of the human body, the components rarely meet at right angles. Modern chair designers tend to tackle this problem by combining straight sections with pre-curved components – as this design does.

This is the first project to introduce wood curving techniques. Curved seat and back pieces are attached to a straight-sectioned frame joined by mortise and tenon joints.

AIMS OF THE PROJECT
Introduce the techniques of shaping timber.

TOOLS YOU WILL NEED
Chalk
Pencil
Rule
Panel saw
Marking gauge
Marking knife
Jack plane
Dovetail saw
Range of chisels
Mortise gauge
Try square
Power router or a rebate
or shoulder plane and a
hand router
Spokeshave
Scraper plane
Sash cramps
Cabinet scraper
Sanding block
Screwdriver
Drill

TIME TO ALLOW
If you have made the previous projects, the underframe of this chair should take two or three weekends, depending upon your power tools. Allow two weekends to make the seat and back.

REMEMBER
Plan your work schedule so that the correct sequence is followed.

HEALTH AND SAFETY
Follow the safe working procedures outlined on page 9.

CHOOSING WOOD

Beech, ash and oak are often used in chairmaking, as a slightly flexible wood is needed. Beech is used specifically in upholstered chairs as it takes tacks and staples well without splitting. Your choice of wood for a single chair will depend on availability, and how and where you wish to use it. For a later project you could make a set of these chairs.

CUTTING LIST		
No	Sawn	Planed
2	BACK LEGS 711mm x 38mm x 38mm 2ft 4in x 1½in x 1½in	686mm x 30mm x 30mm 2ft 3in x 1¼in x 1¼in
2	FRONT LEGS 432mm x 38mm x 38mm 1ft 5in x 1½in x 1½in	380mm x 30mm x 30mm 1ft 3in x 1¼in x 1¼in
2	SIDE RAILS 457mm x 85mm x 25mm 1ft 6in x 3½in x 1in	432mm x 75mm x 22mm 1ft 5in x 3in x ⅞in
3	CROSS RAILS 457mm x 130mm x 25mm 1ft 6in x 5in x 1in	2 @ 406mm x 115mm x 22mm 1ft 4in x 4½in x ⅞in 1@ 280mm x 115mm x 22mm 11in x 4½in x ⅞in
6	TO MAKE SEAT 406mm x 75mm x 25mm 1ft 4in x 3in x 1in	380mm x 75mm x 20mm 1ft 3in x 3in x ¾in
1	TOP BACK RAIL 380mm x 38mm x 38mm 1ft 3in x 1½in x 1½in	368mm x 30mm x 30mm 1ft 2½in x 1¼in x 1¼in
6	VERTICAL SLATS SAWN FROM SOLID 457mm x 75mm x 45mm 1ft 6in x 3in x 1¾in	Several can be sawn from 1 piece
1	CURVED TOP RAIL 380mm x 75mm x 45mm 1ft 3in x 3in x 1¾in	
+ adhesive, screws, masking tape, finishing		

PLANS

The drawings on this page show the elevations and sections, together with an exploded perspective view of the finished piece.

Scale 1:10.5

Curved top rail

Back seat support rail

Top back rail

Side rail

Cross rail

Cross rail

Cross rail

Side rail

Exploded diagram

444mm 1'5½"

375mm 1'3"

68mm 2¾"

22mm 7/8"

25mm 1"

610mm 2"

75mm 3"

22mm 7/8"

234mm 9⅛"

115mm 4½"

280mm 11"

406mm 1'4"

356mm 1'2"

305mm 12"

30mm 1¼"

Centre line

30mm 1¼"

457mm 1'6"

1¼" 30mm

Sectional side elevation through centre line

Front elevation

BUYING TIMBER

1 The timber is in two sizes, the legs being out of 38mm (1½in) material and the rails out of 25mm (1in) material. The seat and back barrel forms are from 25mm (1in) thickness but the top rail that holds the back is out of 38mm (1½in) thickness.

PLANE ALL COMPONENTS

2 Saw the components from the board, plane them all face side, face edge, width and thickness and leave slightly over length.

MARK OUT COMPONENTS

3 Mark out all the components working from the face side and face edge and marking in pencil.

MAKING THE UNDERFRAME

4 Start with the frame before proceeding to work on the seat and back. Mark and cut the underframe components in the following order.

5 The two side rails and the back seat support rail are joined into an H-frame. The back seat support rail is wider than the side rails since it has to have the curve to support the seat cut into it. Mark the curve now, and the decorative curves at the side, and cut outside the line. True the main surface later when the underframe is glued, but work the decorative curves with a spokeshave and scraper. ▼

6 The back seat support rail is joined to the side rails with twin through mortises and tenons. The twin tenon is a decorative feature and forms a stronger joint than a single large mortise and tenon. Mark them in pencil, check they are correct, mark with a cut line then saw and chisel the mortises and tenons.

7 Scrape all flat surfaces. ▶

8 Assemble the H-frame dry. ▶

9 It is convenient at this stage to drill holes in the back and front seat support rails for the counterbored screws that will later hold the seat in place. ▶

10 The front rail and back rail are also joined by twin through mortise and tenon joints to the two side rails of the H-frame.

11 The front rail has to have the curve formed for the seat. Mark the curve and cut outside the line as before. Leave precise finishing until later. Mark and cut the tenons that will fit into the legs on both the front rail and the back rail. Note that the shoulder lengths are not the same on the two rails.

12 Mark four sets of twin tenons on the side rails and their mortises on the front and back rails.

13 Assemble the H-frame and front and back rails dry. ▶

THE LEGS

14 Mark out the front legs and mark and cut the mortises. ▲

15 Dry fit the legs to the front rail. Repeat the process with the two back legs and back rail. ▲

16 Mark and cut the front legs and the bottoms of the back legs to length. Assemble all these components dry; you should now have an underframe that is together, but the back legs have nothing in between them at the top. ▼

CURVING THE SEAT SUPPORTS

17 Take a rule, place it across the front rail and the back seat support rail and mark the angle that you will need to spokeshave on the curved position of those two rails. ▼

ASSEMBLING THE FRAME

18 Even though the legs are now fitted to the frame, do not glue them at this stage. Sand the seat frame and glue this underframe assembly of five pieces together, starting with the initial H-frame and then adding the front and back rails. ▶

MAKING THE SEAT

19 The seat is composed of six slats glued together into a curved form. Prepare these pieces and mark the angles on the edges that will enable the series of slats to form the curve.

20 Cut some spare pieces of wood to the curve of the seat then lay the slats on these and check that the angles when you plane are correct to form the required curve. It can help assembly if you make four of these curved pieces, two male and two female. A pair at the front and back help during cramping.

21 When the slats fit together dry, glue them. Put masking tape on the underside of the curve which holds the bottom edges together and run the glue on the two faces, allowing the masking tape to hinge them open. When you later rest the seat assembly on the female curve all the joints close up.

22 Cramp across the barrel curve of the seat, and it is here that the male and female support curves are handy. G-cramp these lightly to the back and front of the seat and fit small sash cramps across the seat. You should get enough pressure to just squeeze those angled faces together.

23 Remove the glue before it has dried. When the glue has cured take the seat curve out of the cramps and work the seat shape. You can use a plane on the outside of the curve but will have to use a spokeshave on the inside. ▼

24 Mark the taper on the seat from front to back and the slight curves on the front and on the back and saw to these lines. Plane the edges and work the radii on the two sides. Sand the seat all over. ▲

25 Place the seat on the underframe sub-assembly. If necessary, adjust the curve on the front and back seat support rails. ▶

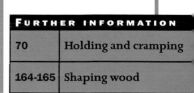

FURTHER INFORMATION	
70	Holding and cramping
164-165	Shaping wood

28 Cut and fit the halving joints but do not glue in position yet. Cut the curve in the top back rail. Mark and cut the slats for the curved top rail. Since these slats will be glued into position, you do not have to make the barrel first but can glue the slats to the curve of the top back rail. Fix the centre slat in position first and then fit and glue the remaining slats. ▶

26 It is useful at this stage to locate the seat and screw it into place. You may have to remove it before finally finishing the chair but it is more manageable this way. ▲

MAKING THE BACK

27 The back legs are fitted to the seat frame dry with a cramp holding them. Mark the top back rail with the halving joints that connect it to the top of the back legs, and mark the curve that will hold the slats that make up the back. ▶

29 Mark and work the shapes on the bottom of the back rail and the radii on the sides of the back rest. ▶

30 Plane the bottom of the slats and the top level with the top back rail. ▲

FINAL ASSEMBLY

31 Sand down all the components. Glue the front legs to the front rail, the back legs to the back rail and the back assembly to the top of the back legs. ▼

32 The finished chair. For a later project you could make a set of these chairs. ▼

Dowel Joints

Dowelling is a traditional technique and is widely used in the craft of chair making. Dowels were sometimes also used in traditional woodwork as pins to hold a mortise and tenon joint.

Dowels can be used for joining chipboard and other manmade boards.

Dowels

For a well-made joint the dowel must fit tightly in the hole and a minimum of 20mm (¾in) of dowel should extend into each piece. The combined depth of the holes should be slightly greater than the dowel length.

You can buy dowels in different diameters and lengths ready-made for jointing. These have grooves cut in the sides to allow air and excess adhesive to escape from the hole as the joint is cramped up. The dowel ends are chamfered to enable them to go more easily into the holes.

MAKING YOUR OWN DOWEL PEGS

It is quite simple and economical to buy a length of dowel rod and cut it into the number of dowels needed for jointing. You are most likely to need dowels of 6mm, 10mm and 12mm (¼in, ⅜in and ½in) diameter.

1 Cut the dowels to length against the bench stop as and when you need them. ▲

2 Use the marking gauge to cut grooves in the dowel to allow air and glue to escape when the joint is cramped up. ▲

3 Alternatively, fix a tenon saw upside down in the bench vice and run the dowel pegs over the teeth to groove them. ▲

4 Chamfer both ends of the dowels for easy entry into the drilled holes. Use a rasp, or buy a dowel rounder, which is rather like a pencil sharpener, turned in a brace or drill while the dowel is held upright in the vice. ▲

MARKING OUT

Like all joints, dowelling relies on precise marking. You can buy jigs to help with marking and drilling, but it is possible to achieve a good match very simply.

Faces to be marked must be flat and square. A minimum of two dowels are necessary for each joint. Larger or heavier work may call for more dowels.

Ensure that the shoulders are flat and square and mark the positions on one component using square, gauge and knife.

1 With the wood held securely in the vice, use the square to mark the dowel centres. Mark from the face side. ▲

2 Set the marking gauge to half the rail thickness, and mark across the centres from the face side. ▲

TRANSFERRING MARKS

1 Use panel pins to transfer marks from one component of the joint to the other. Mark up the hole centres on the first piece of wood and drive a panel pin into each one. ▶

2 Cut the heads off the pins with pliers or cutters. Then align the second piece, then press or tap it down to locate the hole centres. Remove the pins with pliers. ▶

3 Centre points are purpose-made for marking dowel joints. Mark up and drill the holes in the first piece of wood. Insert the centre points and press the second piece into position to transfer the marks. ▶

DRILLING

Once the centres of the holes have been marked, drill the holes using either a brace and bit, a hand drill or power drill.

1 Use a drill with a centre point to locate precisely in the hole centres you have marked. An engineer's twist drill is liable to wander from the centre. ▲

2 It is essential to drill square to the surface and not at an angle. Stand in line with the wood to make sure you are drilling parallel to the sides. Use a depth stop to ensure you drill to the required depth (see right). ▲

DEPTH STOPS

Wood must often be drilled to a specific depth, for example, when making dowel joints or to ensure the drill does not break out on the other side of the wood. You can buy a depth stop to fit around the drill bit, or wind a piece of tape around the drill at the required depth.

Making your own depth stop

Make sure the drill is firmly located in the drill chuck. Decide on the depth of hole and mark that distance on the drill from its end.

Measure from the mark to the chuck and make the stop from a piece of wood the same length. Drill a hole through the wood, the exact diameter of the drill bit. Smooth off the sharp edges to prevent damage to the work, and fit it over the bit. ▲

ASSEMBLING THE JOINT

1 Check that the dowel joint is correctly aligned with a dry run, before adding adhesive. ▲

2 Add the glue to the holes, not the dowels, to prevent the dowels swelling. Use a mallet, or a hammer protected with a piece of waste wood, to tap the joint components together. ▲

Upright Chair

The chair is one of the most challenging items for any furniture designer. An upright chair must be strong enough to withstand many different stresses, yet be light enough to be pulled up to a table or desk.

Many of the traditional solutions to problems posed by chairmaking remain the best, but there are still plenty of opportunities for design variations.

A chair is judged on comfort, and this is not due to the amount of upholstery it has, but to the angles and positions of the individual parts of the chair and the support the frame gives to the body. In a well-designed chair, body muscles don't have to work to maintain a comfortable posture.

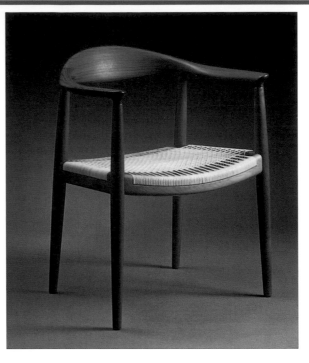

HANS WEGNER • *Chair*
With a seat of woven cane, the flowing back and arms of this chair make it a classic of its kind. Originally designed in 1947, this chair is another example (see right) of Danish mass-produced articles based on the tradition of hand-crafted work. ◀

SUPPORTING THE BODY

In an upright or "working" chair, the body needs support in five places: under the heels, under the pelvic bones, and the lumbar region, or small of the back.

Centre of gravity

The best position for accomplishing tasks, whether eating, writing or typing, is one where the spine is upright with the centre of gravity running down the backbone from the skull to the pelvis.

Principles of body support

Erect posture to accomplish tasks

Lumbar

Pelvis

Centre of gravity from skull down backbone to pelvis

Heel

Basic position

This basic position is maintained whether the person is seated cross-legged on the floor, or in the "Balans" position proposed by Norwegian researchers in the 1980s. In this position, the body weight is shared between the pelvis and the knees. ▼

Oriental

Balans

Chair sizes

Optimum chair sizes to suit the average adult have developed over time, and designers now have a set of dimensions from which they can begin work.

These basic measurements are the starting point for a wide range of design adaptations. The measurements must be adapted to suit anyone who is not of average height and build.

If you are designing a chair to match a table, make sure that the chair will be able to be drawn up to the table. ▶

h=seat height
390mm to 432mm (15½in to 17in)
Always start working from

HANS WEGNER • *China chair*
Hans Wegner has been one of the most prolific and consistent of the Scandinavian designers. Throughout his career he has produced classic, timeless pieces that are still fresh today, 40 years after they were designed. ◀

this measurement. If the chair is too high it presses into the backs of the thighs; if it is too low, it may be difficult to get out of.

p=pelvic support
150mm (6in)
This is the area which supports the weight of the body.

d=seat depth
343mm to 380mm (13½in to 15in)
A chair that is too deep presses on the backs of the legs, while one that is too shallow may be unstable.

r=seat rake
approximately 25mm (1in) or 5 to 8 degrees. The seat is angled down from the horizontal to support the natural tilt of the pelvis and the lumbar curve of the spine. Working and desk chairs are often flat, which makes it easier for the user to lean forward to type or write.

c of l = centre of lumbar
200mm (8in)
The distance from the rear of the seat to the centre of the lumbar area where back support is needed.

l=lumbar region
100mm (4in)
This is the area that should be shaped to follow the lumbar

curve. For a high back, extend this area at an angle of 20 to 25 degrees to the vertical to support the shoulders.

a=arm height from rear of seat
240mm (9½in)
Use this dimension to calculate the height of an arm rest, or the relative height of a table top.

w=width of seat
480mm to 510mm (19in to 20in) between arms 430mm to 460mm (17in to 18in) of seat
Seat width often tapers from front to back to allow room for legs at the front while leaving clearance for elbows at the rear.

JOHN MAKEPEACE WORKSHOPS • *Phoenix chair*
A very dramatic design. Made with a laminated holly bark, with burr elm, bleached and scorched oak, it has a positive presence. The choice of materials greatly enhances the qualities of the chair. ▲

Table height
700mm (2ft 4in)

These final projects apply and develop in different ways the skills you have learnt earlier. The desk has drawers, uses mortise and tenon joints and introduces new carcase construction techniques – frames with panels. You can easily customize the desk design to suit your own requirements. With the fine boxes your woodworking moves onto a different scale. The solid wood box develops craftsmanship with the incorporation of through dovetails. The ply boxes give an opportunity to experiment with varieties and colours of veneer. Finally, the easy chair is a major project, but by now you should not find it difficult since it applies previous knowledge.

Desk

This desk brings together a number of the techniques you have learned and practised in earlier projects.

Making this project demonstrates how a complicated furniture construction is broken down into a series of simpler components – frames, carcases, drawers and framed panels. Each component is made separately then combined in stages into the completed desk.

AIMS OF THE PROJECT
To show how advanced furniture construction is broken down into simpler components.

TOOLS YOU WILL NEED
Chalk
Pencil
Rule
Panel saw
Marking gauge
Marking knife
Jack plane
Dovetail saw
Range of chisels
Mortise gauge
Try square
Power router or a rebate plane or shoulder plane and a hand router
Sash cramps
Cabinet scraper
Sanding block
Drill for screw or dowel assembly, or biscuit jointer; screwdriver

TIME TO ALLOW
The side frames should be completed in one weekend; the modesty board and the top in another weekend each. The drawer frame could take up to two weekends and the drawers one or two weekends. Allow a weekend to assemble and finish.

REMEMBER
Read the instructions and plan the job in your mind.

HEALTH AND SAFETY
Follow the safe working procedures outlined on page 9.

CHOOSING WOOD
With the experience gained on earlier projects you should be able to choose any quality hardwood that is available and that fits in with your decor.

CUTTING LIST

No & Type	Sawn	
1	TOP	
2 long rails	965mm x 57mm x 30mm	3ft 2in x 2¼in x 1¼in
2 short rails	560mm x 57mm x 30mm	1ft 10in x 2¼in x 1¼in
1 sheet	914mm x 510mm x 12mm	3ft x 1ft 8in x ½in ply or MDF
2	SIDE FRAMES	
4 legs	762mm x 45mm x 30mm	2ft 6in x 1¾in x 1¼in
4 rails	533mm x 57mm x 30mm	1ft 9in x 2¼in x 1¼in
1	REAR FRAME	
2 long rails	914mm x 57mm x 30mm	3ft x 2¼in x 1¼in
2 short rails	510mm x 45mm x 30mm	1ft 8in x 1¾in x 1¼in
1 sheet	838mm x 406mm x 10mm	2ft 9in x 1ft 4in x ⅜in ply or MDF
1	DRAWER FRAME	
4 cross rails	914mm x 3 @ 57mm 1 @ 80mm x 25mm	3ft x 3 @ 2¼in 1 @ 3¼in x 1in
3 side rails	510mm x 140mm x 25mm	1ft 8in x 5½in x 1in
8 drawer runners	510mm x 38mm x 25mm	1ft 8in x 1½in x 1in
2	DRAWERS	
2 drawer fronts	432mm x 140mm x 30mm	1ft 5in x 5½in x 1¼in
4 drawer sides	480mm x 100mm x 20mm	1ft 7in x 4in x ¾in
2 drawer backs	432mm x 75mm x 14mm	1ft 5in x 3in x ⅝in
2 drawer bottoms	432mm x 305mm x 6mm	1ft 5in x 12in x ¼in ply or MDF

PLANS

The drawings on this page show the elevations and sections, together with an exploded perspective view of the finished piece.

Scale 1:10

510mm 1'8"

Part plan – section through B-B

25mm 1"

85mm 3½"

50mm 2"

265mm 10½"

457mm 1'6"

20mm 3/4"

128mm 5"

457mm 1'6"

711mm 2'4"

50mm 2"

25mm 1"

12mm ½"

Sectional end elevation through A-A

914mm 3'

Front elevation with part section on C-C

Vertical facing

Exploded diagram

BUYING TIMBER

1 Most of the solid timber is bought sawn at 30mm (1¼in) to finish at 25mm (1in). The drawer unit and drawers use 25mm (1in) or 20mm (¾in) to finish at 20mm (¾in) and 14mm (⅝in). You also need three pieces of ply or MDF.

2 Mark and saw out all components. Then plane them and leave slightly over length.

3 The project is designed in the form of a set of components so the process for each one is described in order.

SIDE FRAMES – MAKE TWO

4 Mark mortise and tenon joints on the four legs and four rails. The rails should have shoulders all round and the top rails a haunch.

5 Cut and fit the joints. Assemble the frames dry, check that they are both the same size and that they are square and flat. Disassemble and sand all the components.▼

6 Reassemble, glue and cramp. Afterwards, give a sanding and a coat of finish.

SURFACE FINISH – TOP AND MODESTY BOARD

7 These finishes should be considered before you make up the panels, and at the same time since they will be seen together.

Linoleum was used for the prototype, since it gives a pleasant writing surface. You can buy ply or MDF that is pre-veneered if you wish to save time. You could also apply your own veneer, lay plastic laminate or paint the surface.

Whichever you choose, the finish should be applied before either panel is inserted in the frame.

MODESTY BOARD – MAKE ONE

8 This is a frame and panel. Mark the vertical stiles and the horizontal rails for the frame and work the groove on the inside faces that will take the panel.

9 Mark and cut all mortise and tenon joints. Remember that the haunches will fill the groove.

10 Assemble the frame dry and mark the ply panel to be a snug fit in the frame. Cut and fit the panel.

11 Disassemble the dry frame, check that the panel fits and everything is square and flat. Glue and cramp it together. When the glue has cured, sand and apply final finish. ▲

TOP – MAKE ONE

12 Cut the board material to slightly over the finished size. The panel has a rebate cut around the edges to fit into grooves in the frame.

13 Mark the four pieces for the frame edging, work the grooves around the inside edges. Mark the top board precisely to its final size, and cut the rebate round all four edges. ▼

14 Begin to apply the four frame pieces to the top board. Care is needed, since the frame corners will be mitred and you are building this frame round the panel. Cut the mitre on the long sides and dry cramp these to the board. Then fit the short ends so that the frame is tight around the board and the four mitres are a good fit. ▼

DRAWER FRAME – MAKE ONE

16 Mark all components. The two side pieces have the cross rails attached to them. The upper front cross rail is wider than the other three since the drawer front sits underneath flush with its edge.

19 Rather than see end grain on the front of the side rails, add a small lipping at the front. ▼

17 Due to the grain direction on the sides, it is not good practice to dovetail these four rails so the four corners are notched. ▲

18 The cross rails are screwed and glued in place. ▼

15 Glue and cramp the frame to the board. After the glue has cured, sand and polish the frame. Set the top aside with the side frames and the modesty board. ▶

FURTHER INFORMATION	
44-45	Making a mortise and tenon joint
47	Preparing the surface
60-61	Finishes
70	Holding and cramping

20 In the centre of the frame a small vertical partition runs from front to back to separate the two drawers. It is notched to the front and back rails, and screwed in place like the ends. This frame is not difficult to make but it is essential to mark out very precisely so that the places where the drawers will run are square and parallel. ▲

21 Add the drawer runners, eight in all. These are fixed by screws in between the four long cross rails and provide a surface on which the drawers slide and run. This component can now be sanded and finished. ▼

DRAWERS MAKE TWO

22 These are made in a similar fashion to previous drawers. Notice that the drawer sides are the complete depth of the drawer frame but the back is located in one-third from the back edge. Drawers should only be pulled out two-thirds of their possible travel, if you pull them right out, they and their contents can end up on the floor.

23 Plane the drawer sides to be a smooth-running fit. Ensure that the back fits the opening precisely. Fit the front. Make grooves in the sides and the front to take the ply bottom. Gauge the thickness of the side on the ends of the back and front. Make twin through tenons between the back and sides and lap dovetails between the front and the sides.

24 Assemble the drawers and fit them in the frame. They should now run sweetly in the drawer frame. ▲

25 Form the drawer handles from routed grooves underneath the drawer fronts, or by cutting spaces in the lower front rail. ▼

OVERALL ASSEMBLY

26 Fit the side frames to the end of the drawer frame and the end of the modesty board. The desk can be assembled permanently using dowels, biscuits or tongues or by screwing the side frames to the desk frame and modesty board.

The prototype was screwed. The advantage of using screws is that if you customize the desk to make it larger, it is much easier to transport the components and assemble them in the room.

27 Screw the side frames at the top from the inside of the drawer frame. ▶

28 The easiest way to screw the modesty board in position is from the outside of the side frames into the end of the drawer frame and the end of the modesty board. The screw heads are then visible in the side frames. Recess the screw heads into a hole and plug that hole if you wish to hide the screws. However, many woodworkers find Posidrive or Allen-head screws are visually quite acceptable. ▶

29 When the basic structure has been assembled, place the top in position and fix it with screws from underneath. Complete the final finish to all components. Slide the drawers into position. ▶

30 The finished desk brings together earlier woodworking techniques and some new ones. ▲

FURTHER INFORMATION	
71	Finishing
86-87	Using a router
94-95	Principles of drawer making

Power Planing

Only hand planing can give you a real "feel" for wood. It is important to master the skill of hand planing first, since it is the only way to understand how the blade cuts, how different timbers and grain directions affect the finish. This feeling is absent when power planing, but machines do remove the hard drudgery of larger jobs.

Anatomy of a power plane
1 Dust bag
2 Sole
3 Handles
4 Cutter block with planer
   knives

POWERED HAND PLANE

This tool cuts with knives held in a revolving cutter block. It is essential to ensure that all guards are properly fitted and that safe procedures are used to ensure that your fingers and hands cannot come near the revolving block.

When you plane an edge with a hand plane, it is often a help to use your leading hand as a guide, holding the side and bottom of the plane. *Never* do this with a power plane.

1 When planing along the grain, keep your hands on both handles. Set the plane to make shallow cuts, and plane slowly for a smooth finish. ▲

You can buy a useful frame to hold the planer with the planing face uppermost to convert it into a machine surfacer or jointer plane. Note the procedures outlined below for using machine planers. Always follow the manufacturer's instructions on the use of guards.

2 If the work is twisted or in wind, take some cuts across the grain. Always take finishing cuts along the grain. ▲

MACHINE PLANES: SURFACING PLANER

The surfacing or jointing planer enables you to plane a surface, a square edge, or an angled edge. Never attempt to plane short material, work should always be 300mm (12in) or longer. ▲

Planing the face side

1 It is important to take the correct stance, standing beside the machine, just behind the cutter block. ▲

2 The machine has guards that ensure you cannot get your hands near the cutter block, either a bridge guard, or one that pivots out of the way when the work is over the block. Always use these guards. ▲

3 Feed the wood from the lower infeed table towards the cutter block, which is set slightly higher. The outfeed table is the same height as the cutter block blades. Depth of cut is adjusted by raising or lowering the infeed table. ▷

4 When feeding the material, which may have some twist in it, put pressure first on the timber on the infeed table. ▷

5 When the block has started to cut, and the work has emerged from under the guard, move your leading hand, and then the other hand, to ensure the work lies flat on the outfeed table. This movement becomes second nature with practice. ▷

Planing an edge

Check first that the fence is square with the table. Make sure all guards are in place, and feed the timber, using the same sequence of movements as planing the face, but this time also ensure that the face side is flat against the fence. ▼

Planing an angle

1 To plane an angle other than 90°, adjust the angle of the fence. Take extra care to ensure that the face side is pressed against the fence. ▼

Anatomy of a thicknessing planer

1. Direction of timber feed
2. Timber to be thicknessed
3. Infeed roller
4. Infeed pressure bar
5. Rotating cutter block
6. Outfeed pressure bar
7. Outfeed roller

THICKNESSING PLANER

1 Once the surfacing planer has smoothed the face side and the face edge, the thicknesser ensures that the work is accurately planed to the required width and then to thickness. The principle is like an old-fashioned mangle.

2 Do not attempt to take too deep a cut. When feeding the work in, always keep your fingers away from the feed aperture. ▲

3 To plane thin material, use a base board. You can easily make one from scrap material. Screw an end batten onto the board to keep it in place. Feed the thin pieces along this false platform. Do not attempt to plane thin material to width. ▼

FURTHER INFORMATION	
9	Safety first
24-25	Planing
76-77	Power hand tools
92-93	Machine tools

Desks

A desk needs a writing surface at a comfortable height, and normally includes some form of storage for writing implements and stationery.

Nowadays desks must accommodate computers and peripheral equipment of varying shapes and sizes. The home office also needs filing and other document storage.

ANDREW LAWTON • *Chevron desk*

A lovely restrained design, with elegant details. The folded panel ends make the most of some lovely figured timber, and the wedged through tenons are well-placed. A fine piece of drawer making with interesting handles, complemented by a subtly coloured top. ▶

Simple desk

The desk is a writing table with one or more drawers. The table surface can be inlaid with some resilient material that feels pleasant to write on. The table top may be flat, or simple storage can be placed along the back. ▶

JUDITH AMES • *Desk (and chair)*

The table is a simple four-leg design, enriched by curves on the legs and on the rails. The contrast between the timbers works well and the whole has a classic, timeless look that will last. ▼

Pedestal desk

A pedestal or kneehole desk takes the writing table one step further with frame and panel sides to create storage areas in one or both sides. ▶

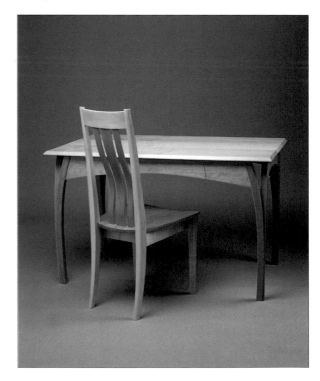

"Partner's desk"

The traditional "partner's desk" is a large, solid and imposing version of the pedestal desk, framed all round. ▶

Bureau

The bureau developed in the 17th century. The sloping fall flap opens to create the writing surface and to reveal a variety of pigeon-holes and storage compartments. When open, the flap is supported by pull-out lopers. The basic idea can be developed with arrangements of drawers or cupboards below and a bookcase on top. ▲

Brass stays

Brass stays are the alternative means of supporting the fall flap. The internal storage is set back slightly to allow for the movement of the stay. Stays may also be curved, or cranked with a hinge in the middle. ▶

Roll-tops

The roll-top desk became popular in America in the 19th century. The tambour, or sliding door, is made of wooden slats glued to a canvas backing. This flexibility enables the tambour to slide around curves. ◀

Workstations

With computers, the desk has become a "workstation" that must provide space for a variety of different pieces of equipment. Keyboards should be placed 50mm (2in) lower than a writing surface to avoid strain, while the monitor may be placed higher, at eye level. ▲

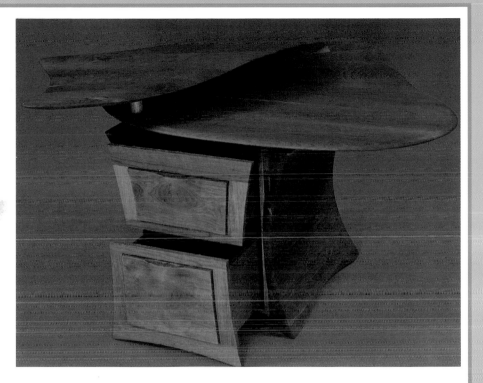

DAVID DELTHONY ● Clam desk
A very interesting sculptural form, with surfaces on two levels, the upper for writing, the lower for keyboard use, both deriving from one folded form. The desk is approached from three sides, one for writing, one for typing and the third for access to the storage drawers. The form of the top, and the shapes of the pedestal complement each other. ▲

FURTHER INFORMATION	
58-59	Principles of cabinet construction
124-129	Module 6: desk

Veneers

Veneers are thin slices of wood, used for decorative or constructional purposes. Wood is converted into decorative veneer because some species are too rare or expensive to be used as solid board, or their structure makes them unsuitable to be used in solid form. When glued to a stable ground, they produce fine colours, shapes, patterns and textures that may be impossible to achieve using solid board.

Do not think of veneer as a substitute, or as giving a lower quality result. Veneer is a viable and respectable alternative to solid wood.

Decorative veneers are usually quite thin 0.6mm to 1mm ($1/64$in to $1/32$in), thick. Constructional veneers are used in the production of plywood or laminated shapes and are generally much thicker, from 2.5mm to 3.5mm ($3/32$in to $1/8$in).

VENEER PRODUCTION

The specialist veneer manufacturer must be able to gauge the likelihood of valuable or interesting veneer that will result from conversion by looking at the uncut log. The expertise of the veneer cutter lies in knowing how to cut the log to produce the greatest quantity of valuable veneer. It is possible to cut large sheets from some timbers but in timber with unusual features, the veneer sheets will be quite small. There are three main methods of cutting veneer: rotary cut, sliced and sawn.

PARTS OF THE TREE

The largest volume of veneer is produced from the main trunk. Other parts of the tree are used for special grain or patterned effects: the crotch, the stump or areas of burr. Veneer is generally cut along the grain, but "oysters" may be cut from slices across the grain, to produce striking end grain patterns.

Crotch

Main trunk

Burr

Stump

Saw cutting

Before the development of veneer slicing machines in the eighteenth century, all veneers were cut by sawing. Now sawing is only used for particular species or logs that are difficult to peel or slice, or where a particular grain feature can only be obtained by sawing.

Saw cutting is very wasteful. Up to 50 per cent of the log may be lost in the saw cut. ▲

Rotary cutting

The log is first softened by soaking in water, or steaming. A large knife is set to cut the veneer to the required thickness, assisted by a pressure bar which helps the veneer part evenly.

The log is held between centres, and rotated against the knife to produce a continuous sheet of veneer.

Knife

The knife is set forward of the pressure bar by the required thickness of the veneer. ▲

Veneer cut from a half-round log is narrower, but has a similar figure to veneer produced by off-centre cutting. ▲

This is an efficient method for producing large sheets for plywood and laminates; it is also used for some decorative veneers, particularly to produce the bird's-eye effect in maple.

Rotary cutting produces veneer with a distinctive pattern produced by the tangential cut through the growth rings.

Mounting the log off-centre produces a wide veneer, but with a decorative grain figure. ▲

In back cutting the log is mounted with heartwood facing outwards to produce decorative figures such as burrs and curls. ▲

Slicing

This method produces decorative hardwood veneers. The log is first cut lengthways and its grain assessed to determine how further cuts can produce the most interesting or valuable veneers.

The log is further cut into "flitches" which are mounted on a sliding frame. As the frame moves down it pushes the wood against the knife blade and pressure bar to slice off a sheet of veneer.

The flitch can be mounted in several different ways to produce various grain patterns.

Flat-sliced veneer may also be cut tangentially from a quartered log, this produces narrow but attractive veneers. ▲

Flat slicing is the most common method, and produces traditional crown-cut veneer with bold curves and ovals. ▲

TYPES OF VENEER

Decorative veneers are always cut to maximize the attractive features of the timber species.

Veneers are stacked in sequence from the slicer to enable patterns to be matched, and they are then sold in sequence. To match up veneers, always take them consecutively from the pack.

Veneer can be commercially coloured, subtly or in vivid hues; lines, bandings and readymade patterns are also available.

Stringing lines are fine strips used to divide different areas of veneer.

Decorative bandings are made from side grain sections glued together

then sliced into strips. Always buy enough of each pattern to complete a project as you may not be able to obtain the exact colour and pattern again.

Inlay motifs are bought readymade to inset in a veneer surface or for use in marquetry. If possible the inlay should be the same thickness as the veneer for even pressure during glueing. Traditionally, other materials like mother of pearl and brass have also been used for veneer inlay.

Veneers, inlays and bandings
1 Aspen
2 Coloured pine
3 Tropical olive
4 Olive ash
5 Brazilian rosewood
6 Cherry
7 Zebrano
8 Pomelle
9 A selection of different inlay motifs
10 Patterned bandings and stringings

FURTHER INFORMATION	
146-147	Laying veneer
166-169	Bending and laminating

Fine Boxes

Precision marking and working are more important than ever when making small objects because our eyes are drawn to look closely at joints, the way things are put together, and the detailing.

The first box is made in solid wood, and has through dovetailing as a structural and visual feature. The second box is veneered and relies for its effect on the choice of veneer.

CHOOSING WOOD

Only a small quantity is needed for the solid box so choose an exciting and exotic wood. The prototype is made out of yew because, although it is difficult to work, it has a lovely appearance.

The veneered box is constructed from ply. Again, not much material is needed so you can choose some really interesting veneers that have patterns on a suitable scale.

CUTTING LIST: SOLID WOOD BOX		
No	Sawn	Planed
TO CUT AND MAKE 4 SIDES, 2 LONG & 2 SHORT		
1	660mm x 85mm x 20mm	2 @ 180mm x 75mm x 12mm
		2 @ 130mm x 75mm x 12mm
	2ft 2in x 3½in x ¾in	2 @ 7in x 3in x ½in
		2 @ 5in x 3in x ½in
1	TO MAKE TOP	
	180mm x 130mm x 20mm	162mm x 115mm x 14mm
	7in x 5in x ¾in	6½in x 4½in x ⅝in
1	TO MAKE BOTTOM	
	180mm x 130mm x 12mm	162mm x 115mm x 10mm
	7in x 5in x ½in	6½in x 4½in x ⅜in
+ masking tape, adhesive, finishing, panel or veneer pins, hinges (optional)		

CUTTING LIST: VENEERED BOX		
No	Sawn	Planed
TO CUT 4 SIDES		
1 ply	320mm x 120mm x 10mm	After wood strip set in to
	12½in × 4¾in × ⅜in	ply at top/bottom division
1 solid	320mm x 12mm x 10mm	line
wood	12½in × ½in × ⅜in	4 @ 76mm × 130mm
		× 10mm
		4 @ 3in × 5in × ⅜in
TO MAKE TOP AND BOTTOM		
2 ply	78mm x 78mm x 10mm	76mm x 76mm x 10mm
	3⅛in × 3⅛in × ⅜in	3in × 3in × ⅜in
FOR INSIDE AND OUTSIDE		
2 sheets veneer, not less than		
	480mm × 150mm × 1mm	19in × 6in × 1/32in

PLANS

The drawings on this page and overleaf show the elevations and sections, together with exploded perspective views of the finished pieces.

Scale 1:3

Lid – drop-on or hinged

Top and bottom fit into grooves prior to assembly

Dovetails

Exploded diagram

Plan

180mm 7"

130mm 5"

Front elevation

75mm 3"

Sectional end elevation

10·5mm 7/16"

115mm 4½"

14mm 5/8"

53mm 2⅛"

100mm 4"

110mm 4⅜"

10mm 3/8"

Arrangement of dovetails
Scale 1:1.5

Dotted line represents the original shape of the sides before the assembled box is angled

FURTHER INFORMATION	
12-15	The nature of wood
30-31	Reading drawings

Construction detail

The carcase sides can be arranged like this when inserting the solid timber strip that hides the ply edges when the lid is opened

Plan

68mm 2¾"

56mm 2¼"

10mm ³/₈"   10mm ³/₈"

Scale 1:2.5

10mm ³/₈"

56mm 2¼"

37mm 1½"

12mm ½"

106mm 4¼"

114mm 4½"

Cutting line

4mm ⅛"

Front elevation

76mm 3"

126mm 5"

Cutting line

Side elevation

Cutting line

Top of lid

Sides of lid

Cutting line

Sides of carcase

Bottom of carcase

Exploded diagram

SOLID DOVETAILED BOX

1 Mark the components on the timber and saw them. Plane all components and cut them slightly over length.

JOINING THE SIDES

2 Work out the size and proportions of the dovetails on the four corners. The prototype has dovetails which diminish in size from one edge to the other, but you could choose any pattern. The box is constructed square, and the sides planed at an angle afterwards.

3 Make cut lines around the shoulders and the ends. Make a pencil line 1.5mm (1/16in) outside the cut lines and saw the sides to that length.

4 The bottom and top of the box have mitres. These mitres allow the grooves that hold the top and bottom to be worked without them showing at the corners, the mitre covering the grooves. Check your marking out then work the grooves.

MARKING AND CUTTING DOVETAILS

5 Cut the pins first and mark the tails from them. On the two short sides that are to receive the pins, very carefully mark the dovetails on the end grain, pencil in the parts that will be waste and put a cut line and gauge line across the end and down the sides to the shoulder line. ▼

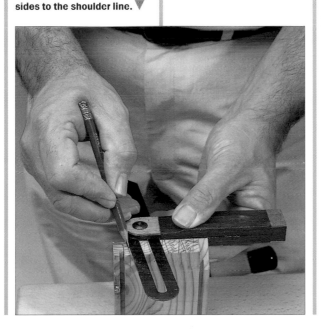

6 Cut the pins, sawing down the waste side of the line to the shoulder line in each case. Saw out the waste with a coping saw. ▼

7 Carefully pare the shoulders. Do this on each of the four corners. ▶

8 With the long sides on the bench, the inside face uppermost, position the cut pins and mark the tails from them. It may be worth using a cramp to ensure that the pieces do not move. ▲

FURTHER INFORMATION	
26	Chiselling
26-27	Sawing
68-69	Making dovetail joints

9 Mark the waste with a pencil and cut to the waste side of the lines you have just marked with a dovetail saw and then cut out the waste with a coping saw. Pare to the shoulder lines.

10 You cannot try the joints dry until you have cut the mitres, two on each corner. Mark the mitres with a cut line and saw about 1.5mm ($^1/_{16}$in) away from this line so that you can tap the joint together and fit each corner, paring where necessary.

11 When the joints are fitted and it looks as if they will go together well, finally cut the mitres. You should now have four sides to the box, joined by the dovetails, but dry without glue. ▲

MAKING THE TOP AND BOTTOM

12 Cut the top and bottom precisely, remembering to allow for the overlap and the tongues that will fit in the grooves on the box sides. Mark out accurately and plane the bottom and top to size. Work the grooves that will allow them to fit into the grooves in the sides.

13 The box top has a curved face, work that now. Also make the bevel on the top sides and, if you wish, the internal carving on the inside of the lid. It is not essential, but is often done with small boxes to lessen the weight of the top. ▲

14 Disassemble the four sides and check the fit of all parts. Sand and polish all inside surfaces, making sure you mask the joint surfaces of the dovetails. You can, however, polish the grooves in the sides and top and bottom since the construction here allows for a slight movement of the wood in the top and bottom in the frame. ▼

15 Glue the joints and assemble the box, removing from the cramps when the glue has cured. Plane the outsides from their original rectangular shape, this gives the box some interest, especially in the apparent reduction in the size of the dovetails.

16 Gauge a line around the completed box where you wish the lid to separate from the bottom. ▼

17 Saw the top from the bottom. ▲

18 Plane the joining surface so that the top fits the bottom exactly. ▼

MAKING THE BOX LININGS

19 Linings fit inside the box and are mitred at the corners. They need careful planing since they should be as tight as possible without allowing them to bow. Finally, polish the box. ▼

20 The prototype is made with a simple drop-on top but if you wish you can fit hinges.

21 The finished box sealed and waxed, to bring out the grain. ▶

VENEERED PLY BOX

1 Purchase your veneer and some 10mm (⅜in) ply wood. Mark out and cut the components. You should have two squares for the top and bottom and one piece from which four sides will later be cut.

2 When you cut the lid from the bottom, that cut will expose ply on the joint faces. The box will look much better if, when it is opened, only solid timber is visible. So, before you do any work on the joints, make a cut approximately where you wish the lid to separate on the piece that represents the four sides and glue in a strip of wood. ▲

3 You can make the insert slightly thicker than the ply but make sure that the ply is perfectly flat when re-glued. When the glue has cured, plane the insert down so that the piece is flat again.

4 Cut the four side pieces. You now need to apply the inside veneer to these sides and the two top/bottoms. This small job can be easily accomplished by pressing the ply and veneer between two blocks. Always put polythene between the outside face of the veneer and the block.

5 When the glue has cured, remove from the cramps, trim the veneer, sand and finish the inside surfaces. ▲

6 Carefully cut the six pieces to the exact size and join them using a very simple lap joint. Check that the box goes together dry. Glue the corner faces. ▼

7 Bring the four sides together and use panel pins or veneer pins to assemble the box. Be careful that the pins do not go through the inside face. It is useful, with the pins holding the parts in position, to cramp the four pieces in the vice or in a G-cramp to ensure a tight fit. ▲

8 Check that the four-sided box is square. ▶

9 Before gluing on the top and bottom, remove the excess glue from inside the box. ▶

10 Glue and pin the top and bottom to complete a six-sided box. You will not be able to remove the glue from the inside of the top and bottom until later, but because the inside surfaces have been finished, this should not be difficult. ▼

11 Punch the heads of the pins below the ply surface. ▶

12 Plane the six outside faces, ensuring that each is flat and parallel with its opposite side. ▼

13 Mark with a large "T" which of the two ends is the top surface because otherwise you will not know where the timber insert is located when you cut the top from bottom. Make sure you have a diagram or pattern which tells you exactly where this insert is.

14 Apply veneers to the outsides. First take two of the opposite rectangular faces and apply the veneer. ▼

15 Cramp the box. Use off-cuts as protective blocks to protect the veneered surface during cramping. ▲

16 When these veneers have cured, very carefully trim the veneer all round paying special attention to the four long edges.

17 Repeat the process so that all four sides are veneered. Trim again. ▶

18 Mark with a cut line where you will separate top and bottom since, as soon as you apply the end veneer, you will lose your "T" mark. Glue the veneer to the top and bottom. Trim the veneer very carefully, sand all over and apply the first finishing coat.

19 Re-mark the position of the lid and cut the lid from the bottom. ▼

20 Carefully plane the finished rim so both sides fit. ▲

21 The lid is located in position by dowels at the four corners. First mark the position of the dowels in the lid. ▼

22 Using pins transfer these marks to the box bottom. Drill and fit top dowels, and drill corresponding holes in the bottom. ▼

23 Check all over and apply final polish. ▲

24 The finished box, polished to a rich glow. ▼

Laying Veneer

One of the thrills of woodworking is to use solid wood. However, some wood is too expensive or has grain that is unsuitable to work in solid form. Many exotic timbers are only available as veneer.

In industry veneers are applied in a hydraulic press with heated platens. Traditional woodworkers make a hand press or "caul" to do a similar job. The technique described here shows how to lay and press veneer with a simple handmade caul.

Veneer can also be applied by hand using animal glue, laying the veneer with a special veneer hammer. This is a very skilled technique and is usually limited to restoration or replica-making.

APPLYING LIPPING

Lippings are generally applied to manufactured board that is to be veneered, and can be solid wood or veneer. They can be attached in a range of ways: glue only; tongue and groove; loose tongue or biscuit.

Glue only

Tongue and groove

Loose tongue or biscuit.

You can veneer first then lip, in which case the veneers will show.

Or you can lip the board first and finally apply veneer, in which case the lippings will not be seen.

LAYING AND PRESSING

1 Careful preparation is necessary. The ground or face on which the veneer is going to be laid should be flat and clean. You can roughen the surface slightly with a saw blade to provide a key for the adhesive. ▲

2 If jointing is needed to make the sheets of veneer wide enough, the joint must be precise. Clamp the veneer between two boards and plane the edges straight. ▲

3 Use paper tape to hold joints together. Masking tape is too thick, and transparent tape, while it is useful because of its transparency, can lift the grain when it is removed (unless it is a special low-tack type). ▼

4 The veneer must be cut slightly oversize, about 12mm (½in) extra all round, so mark this cutting line on the veneer using a pencil. ▼

5 Cut veneer with a sharp marking knife against a steel straight edge. Cut about 3mm (⅛in) outside the pencil line, and cut across the grain first as this is most likely to split. ▲

6 If pieces of veneer must be cut and jointed, do this first then lay on the ground in one piece. ▲

10 Lay the veneer, smoothing it down by hand. Then with a clean roller, press it down, working from the centre to the edges. The principle with veneer laying is always to squeeze adhesive from the centre outwards and ensure that no air is trapped. ▼

7 Make the caul or press from two substantial boards or sheets of blockboard, chipboard or MDF at least 25mm (1in) thick and larger than the panel to be veneered. Do not use jointed boards for the caul. ▲

9 The choice of adhesive is important. Use either PVA or UR. It is not generally advisable to use contact adhesive for natural timber. Only use this when laying surfaces like plastic laminates or linoleum. Metal surfaces, tiles and mosaics need special adhesives.

Apply adhesive to the ground only and not to the veneer. It is worth spreading the adhesive with a roller to obtain a film of consistent thickness. ▼

11 Large G-cramps will give enough pressure on a small job. But because of the depth of throat on most G-cramps, there will not be enough pressure on the centre of the caul. ▼

12 On a larger job use battens, cut to a slight curve, on the outside of the caul. Then when the cramps are tightened, pressure is applied first to the centre of the caul. ▲

13 Allow enough time for the adhesive to have thoroughly cured before opening the press.

The time will depend on the type of glue used, but overnight is always preferable, except if you are using hardeners or accelerators to part cure the adhesive. Keep the workshop at a reasonable temperature, 15.5-21°C (60-70°F).

Trim the veneer with a sharp marking knife, remove any paper tape with a little warm water, and then sand lightly before applying a finish. ▶

8 It is a good idea to finish and wax the inside surfaces of the caul. With some veneers the adhesive can weep through and may stick to the caul. For the same reason always place paper or clean polythene sheet between the caul and the veneer. ▲

FURTHER INFORMATION	
9	Safety first
70	Holding and cramping
134-135	Veneers

Hingeing

A wide range of hinges is available to the woodworker. Most work needs good quality hinges, the best being solid drawn brass butt hinges. The technique illustrated here shows the procedure for fitting hinges to a box, but the same principles apply to hanging doors.

First decide where to place the hinges on the edge of the box. Arrange them not too near the end, but in a position about equal to the hinge length from the corner. Three or more hinges may be necessary for larger boxes or chests.

Types of hinge

Butt hinge

Door lift-off hinge

Back-flap hinge

FITTING HINGES

1 Measure from the end and make a knife mark at this position on either the top or bottom of the box. Then carefully mark the hinge length from the hinge itself. ▲

2 The centre of the hinge pin should be positioned exactly at the corner edge of the bottom and top. Your marking must ensure the hinge is in this exact position. ▲

3 From the first knife location marks, square cut lines on the closing face and outside edge. ▼

4 Then with the two parts held together transfer these marks to the other part. Make an approximate pencil mark to prevent the cut lines going too far down the outside of the box. ▼

5 Set your marking gauge to the exact width of the hinge, measuring from the inside edge of the hinge to the centre of the hinge pin. ▲

6 Gauge the hinge widths from the outside edges on the closing faces of both top and bottom. ▲

7 Re-set the gauge to the thickness of the hinge from its face to the centre of the pin and gauge these lines from the closing faces on the outside edge of the box top and bottom. ▼

8 Notice that the thickness of the hinge at the edge of the web is smaller than the distance from the face to the pin centre. The section you will remove to set the hinge into must be slightly sloped. ▼

9 To remove most of the waste wood, carefully saw a series of cuts at an angle between the two gauge lines. ▲

10 Carefully chop a series of chisel cuts across the grain from the gauge line at the rear of the closing face to a depth on the inside hinge edge equal to the thickness of the hinge. ▲

11 Carefully pare the waste. You should now have a recess into which the hinge fits very snugly and which should be a perfect match on the top and bottom. ▼

12 Place the hinge in position in the recess and mark the exact centre of one of the screw holes, drill a pilot hole and insert one steel screw. ▼

13 Set in both the hinges to the lid first. Then you should be able to offer up that part to the bottom and mark, drill and screw the hinge in position using only one screw in each leaf. ▲

14 You can now test that the lid closes properly and if you need to make any slight adjustments, screw holes that have not been marked yet will enable you to easily re-position. Drill the pilot holes for the remaining screws. ▲

15 Remove the hinges, and plane a slight chamfer on the sharp hinge edges of the box. This ensures the lid can swing freely. ▶

16 Insert all the brass screws into the hinges on the lid first. The final appearance is always improved by aligning the screw slots in one direction. On very fine work, polish the brass hinges with very fine abrasive paper followed with brass polish.

When using brass hinges, you need brass screws, but never insert a brass screw initially. Always insert a steel screw of the same gauge and length first, remove this and insert the brass screw. This is because brass is softer than steel and in difficult and hard timber it is easy to break off the screw head. Always lubricate screws, but especially brass ones, with petroleum jelly, wax, candle wax or soap. ▶

FURTHER INFORMATION	
9	Safety first

Boxes

Boxes and other small items give you an opportunity to explore the use of many different and exotic timbers that may be too scarce or expensive to use for larger pieces.

Work at this scale needs very careful consideration of scale and proportion. Always make full-size drawings of any project. For unusual shapes it is worth making a model in card.

Your work will be handled and studied closely, so think very carefully about any structural and decorative details that you wish to add.

MAKING SOLID TIMBER BOXES

Solid timber boxes can be made in any size. The interior can be fitted out with a range of removable trays and fixed or movable compartments.

The box top can drop on, or it can be hinged in different ways, and have a range of locks and catches fitted. Buy good quality fittings for your work, even though they may be expensive. Cheap, poorly made hardware can be troublesome and spoil the look of an otherwise beautiful piece of work. Solid or extruded brass fittings are superior to folded or pressed brass.

Make the corner joints a feature of the work by using decorative through dovetails. They can be given added emphasis by combining different timbers in a single box. The proportion and arrangement of the pins and tails is a matter of individual choice. Fullsize working drawings will help you to plan the joints.

Different approaches
Shown here, a range of different ways of approaching boxes: jewellery box, blanket chest; dovetail variations for decorative effect. ▼ ▶

For a jewellery box, add hinges, a lock and trays.

ROBERT INGHAM • *Jewellery box*
A beautifully simple jewellery box finely made in English walnut, with burr ash and tulipwood. The top opens in a particularly interesting way. ▲

Through dovetail joints can be made in different patterns.

Blanket chest, using wide boards.

PLYWOOD BOXES

Plywood boxes joined with simple lap joints can be any shape you choose. The material is stable, relatively inexpensive and quick to work with power tools – the limits are only your time and imagination.

Using lap joints means the construction method is hidden, so boxes of this kind are ideal for experimenting and developing your skills and finishes and veneers. As well as exotic timber veneers, there are manmade and coloured veneers. You could also use decorative bandings and inlays.

Consider each box as a complete shape, quickly-made card models will often give you a better idea of the likely success of a design than a drawing.

Use laminating and bending techniques to introduce curves and even circles.

ANDREW WHATELEY ● *Display case*
The shell concept was arrived at by considering how to display and store a set of antique spoons. The fit between the two halves and the hingeing mechanism show precision woodworking, and the shaping and finishing is exquisitely achieved. ▲

NIC PRYKE ● *Veneered box*
A very interesting veneered box which demonstrates skill in making and imagination in conception and development.

Rectangular shape

Square shape

Polygonal shape

Vary the proportions of polygons.

Triangular and tapering shapes.

Pyramid

Use veneers or laminates to create curves.

Lightweight veneers can be bent round in one.

Laminates or heavier veneers need making in two halves, either circular or elliptical.

A decorative tongue and groove joint makes a feature of the join.

Use bending and laminating techniques to make sculptural boxes.

FURTHER INFORMATION

| 136-145 | Module 7: fine boxes |

Easy Chair

This chair calls for two different shaping techniques: shaping curved rails from solid wood, and making curved slats from laminate strips. You can buy construction veneer for the laminate, or cut your own.

The chair is comfortable as it is, but can also have a seat cushion made of leather or fabric filled with feathers.

AIMS OF THE PROJECT
To learn about shaping and laminating.

TOOLS YOU WILL NEED
Chalk
Pencil
Rule
Steel rule at least 610mm (2ft) long
Panel saw
Bowsaw, jigsaw or bandsaw
Marking gauge
Marking knife
Try square
Jack plane
Mortise gauge
Dovetail saw
Range of chisels
Spokeshave
Rasps
Rifflers for shaping arms
Power router or a rebate plane or shoulder plane and a hand router
Sash cramps
Cabinet scraper
Sanding block
Screwdriver
Drill

TIME TO ALLOW
Allow at least four or five weekends.

REMEMBER
When laminating ensure that each piece is kept in the former long enough for the adhesive to cure fully. Marking curves is difficult to do single-handed. You will need to call on a helper briefly for step 11.

HEALTH AND SAFETY
Follow the safe working procedures outlined on page 9.

CHOOSING THE WOOD

The design calls for "sturdy" looking timber. Timber with too fine a grain would be less appropriate than woods like oak, ash, teak, beech or elm. The prototype was made in cherry. Your choice may be affected by the material for the laminated back slats. If you buy constructional veneer your choice will be limited by the species available, but if you intend to cut and plane your own veneer there will be no such limitation.

No	Sawn	Planed
2	BACK LEGS 838mm x 50mm x 50mm 2ft 9in x 2in x 2in	787mm x 45mm x 45mm 2ft 7in x 1¾in x 1¾in
2	FRONT LEGS 560mm x 50mm x 50mm 1ft 10in x 2in x 2in	508mm x 45mm x 45mm 1ft 8in x 1¾in x 1¾in
3	CURVED CROSS RAILS 610mm x 75mm full x 60mm 2ft 3in full x 2½in	572mm x 75mm x 30mm 1ft 10½in x 3in x 1¼ on curve
2	SIDE RAILS AND 2 ARMS 4 @ 686mm x 75mm full x 30mm 2ft 3in x 3in full x 1¼in	660mm x 75mm x 25mm 2ft 2in x 3in x 1in
7	SEAT SLATS 533mm x 57mm x 20mm 1ft 9in x 2¼in x ¾in	from 521mm x 50mm x 14mm 1ft 8½in x 2in x ⅝in
6	BACK SLATS 762mm x 50mm x 12mm 2ft 6in x 2in x ½in	

Each to be laminated from 8 veneers 762mm x 50mm x 1.5mm
2ft 6in x 2in x 1/16in total of 48 required.

+ For lamination former: joinery softwood approx 762mm x 150mm x 60mm (2ft 6in x 6in x 2½in); large sheet of paper, or graph paper, for full-size drawing of back slats; polythene sheets; screws; adhesive

PLANS

The drawings on this page and overleaf show the elevations and sections, together with an exploded perspective view of the finished piece.

Top cross rail

Seat cross rail

Slots in frame

Rebate

Front cross rail

Side rail

Exploded diagram

Enlarge this template to fullsize on graph or squared paper. Then transfer the outline to a piece of softwood to make the lamination former. Each square equals 25mm (1in).

Template for the curved laminates

28
27
26
25
24
23
22
21
20
19
18
17
16
15
14
13
12
11
10
9
8
7
6
5
4
3
2
1
O

FURTHER INFORMATION	
30-31	Reading drawings
108-109	Chairs and their construction

Half plan

669mm 2'2¾"

45 mm 1¾"

38mm 1¼"
50mm 2"
38mm 1¼"
50mm 2"
38mm 1¼"

25mm 1"
50mm 2"
25mm 1"
50mm 2"
25mm 1"
50mm 2"

57mm 2¼"

30mm 1¼"

57mm 2¼"

25mm 1"

57mm 2¼"

Scale 1:8.5

45 mm 1¾"

6mm ¼"

45 mm 1¾"

598mm 1'11½"

75mm 3"

6mm ¼"

787mm 2'7"

25mm 1"

75mm 3"

75mm 3"

75mm 3"

63mm 2½"

500 mm 1'8"

125mm 5"

Front elevation

508mm 1'8"

185mm 7¼"

406mm 1'4"

Sectional side elevation through centre line

45 mm 1¾"

45 mm 1¾"

1 Prepare all wood except back slats to face side, face edge, width and thickness.

3 Mark the tenons on the end of the cross rails, side rails and the arms. The tenons on the side rail have shoulders all round. Mark the through mortises on the side rail that will accept the twin through tenons on the seat cross rail. These through mortises run with the grain for strength. The seat cross rail is set low in the side rail.

5 Cut the mortise and tenon joints for the two side frames. Also cut the mortises for the cross rails. When working through mortises, mark and out from both sides. ▲

SHAPE THE ARMS

6 Each arm is set so that the inside face is in line with the inside surfaces of the legs and the outside edge protrudes. To begin shaping the end, drill a hole to make the inner curve at the end of the arm and saw into the hole.

SIDE FRAMES

2 Mark the lengths of the legs. Mark the positions of the mortises for the side rails, the arms, and the mortises that will take the top and front cross rails. All mortises into the legs are blind, or stopped, mortises. ▲

4 Check the marking and make cut lines and gauge lines where you intend to cut. Remember that you are making a matching pair of frames, right and left.

7 Finish the shape with rasps, files and abrasive paper. You can be more adventurous with this shaping if you wish. ▲

FURTHER INFORMATION	
44-46	Making a mortise and tenon joint
164-165	Shaping wood

DRY ASSEMBLY

8 Assemble both frames dry and check that the frames are square and out of wind and that the joints are tight. Then disassemble and sand the four sides of the arm and side rail and the two inside surfaces of each leg. ▼

GLUE, CRAMP AND FINISH

9 Glue up both frames, cramp and remove excess glue. When the glue has cured, remove from cramps, sand and apply a coat of finish, ensuring that you mask the faces of the joints where the cross rails will be fitted.

THREE CROSS RAILS

10 These rails should be planed all round but will be oversize on thickness to allow for cutting the curves on the front and back. Mark the rails to length, both sides and tenon lengths.

11 Mark the curves with a pencil. It is sufficient to bend a steel rule between the two end points and the centre mark. It helps to have a partner to hold the rule on the centre mark and pencil the line. ▶

12 Trim the ends of all three rails to the overall rail thickness and pencil mark the tenons. ▼

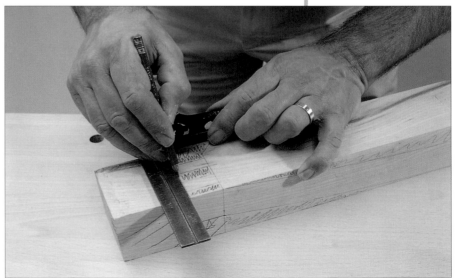

13 Saw the curve. If you only have hand tools use a bowsaw or a coping saw, but this is a slow process. Alternatively use a power jigsaw or a bandsaw. ▶

14 The three rails have a planed surface top and bottom, square ends marked ready for the tenons, and a sawn curve on the outside and inside faces. The curved surfaces must now be completed. Clean up the outside curve with a plane, except at the ends near the tenons which will have to be pared. Smooth the inside curve with a spokeshave.

MARK AND CUT JOINTS IN THE CURVED RAILS

15 The top cross rail has a simple tenon on each end that fits into the mortise on the top of the back legs. Mark out the mortises on the underside of this rail to accept the six back slats. Mark out, check and cut these joints. ▶

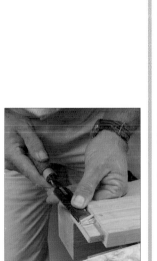

16 The front cross rail has two simple tenons that fit into the front leg. Mark and cut the tenons now. Later this rail will need a bevel at the top edge, which is best marked when the whole frame is assembled dry. It will also need to have recesses cut to receive the seat slats, but this is best done after the slats have been located into their fanned position.

17 The seat cross rail has twin through tenons that fit into the side rails. The shoulders on these tenons are longer than on the other two rails. The underside of this rail sits partly below the side rail and the tenons are made near the top of the seat cross rail to allow for this. Mark and cut these tenons.

18 Fit all the above joints, number or letter them, sand the rails and assemble the whole frame dry. ▼

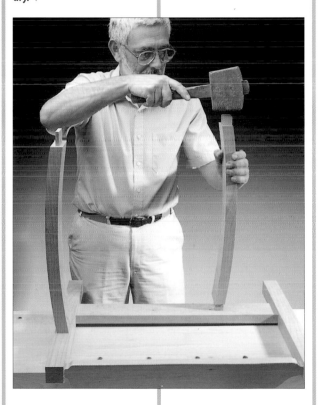

19 With a rule placed between the seat cross rail and the front cross rail measure how much bevel is needed on the front rail. Mark with a pencil, remove the front cross rail, and work the bevel with a plane. Reassemble.

FURTHER INFORMATION	
70	Holding and cramping
76-77	Power hand tools
164-165	Shaping wood

LAMINATED BACK SLATS

20 Make the former from a spare piece of wood. Enlarge the drawing of the back slats to full size. Do this with graph paper or by making a grid of squares and plotting the points where the lines of the curve cross. Transfer this shape to the centre of the former, and cut the shape with a bowsaw, jigsaw or bandsaw. Clean up the faces.

CONSTRUCTIONAL VENEERS

21 If you purchase these, aim for a thickness of between 1.5mm ($\frac{1}{16}$in) and 3mm ($\frac{1}{8}$in). The number you need for each laminated slat will depend on this thickness since the slat will have a finished thickness of 12mm ($\frac{1}{2}$in). Each veneer strip should be 838mm x 57mm wide (2ft 9in x 2$\frac{1}{4}$in). Cut the strips with a craft knife against a steel rule. ▼

22 Alternatively, if you have the machines, you can make your own veneers. Plane a piece of timber 838mm (2ft 9in) long x 57mm (2$\frac{1}{4}$in) thick x a convenient width. Cut a strip off the side planed face 57mm x 3mm (2$\frac{1}{4}$in x $\frac{1}{8}$in) plus. Reface the sawn side on the piece and cut another strip. Repeat refacing and cutting until you have the number of strips needed. They will have one face and two edges planed and one face sawn. Use the thicknessing planer to plane the strips to 3mm ($\frac{1}{8}$in) thickness. Make a baseboard to support the thin strips safely.

23 If your constructional veneers are 3mm ($\frac{1}{8}$in) thick, you need four to make each slat. Try these dry in the former to check that when cramped they are pressed closely together and, if necessary, adapt the mould faces. ▲

APPLY ADHESIVE TO THE VENEERS

24 The adhesive needs to be capable of holding laminates, so either use urea formaldehyde, or one of the stronger formulated PVAs. Apply the adhesive to all internal surfaces, not the two outer outside ones, and ensure coverage by using a glue roller. ▶

LAMINATES IN JIG

25 Wrap the glued bundle of laminates in polythene so that they do not stick to the mould when the glue squeezes out. ▼

26 Place the bundle in the mould and tighten the sash cramps. Try to ensure that the veneers stay in line. The less neat the package, the more you will have to trim off and the result might not be wide enough for your needs. ▶

27 To ensure an even pressure, you will need five cramps, three on the underside and two placed on the top of the former after the first squeeze. ▶

28 When the adhesive has cured (make sure you allow enough time for this) remove from the former. This is a process that you could do each evening during the week, since it is only possible to make one laminate at a time in the one former, and it should cure overnight. ▶

FURTHER INFORMATION

| 70 | Holding and cramping |

29 Plane one of the laminate edges, using the former as a support. ▲

30 Alternatively, hold the laminate in the vice. ▼

31 Gauge the laminate strip to width. ▲

32 Saw to the gauged line and plane the last edge. The laminate is now ready for fitting into the frame. ▼

FITTING BACK SLATS INTO THE FRAME

33 Make the tenons on the top of the back slats to fit into the mortises cut in the underside of the top cross rail (step 15).

Mark the top shoulder line of each tenon from the former. If you do not ensure that the line is marked on each slat in the correct place at the correct end, the curves will not line up when assembled.

Cramp the slats together to mark the tenons. Cut the tenons. The shoulder lines are not yet at the correct angle, you will mark and cut this when you place each slat in its fanned position on the chair frame. ▲

34 Push the tenoned slats into the mortises on the top rail. ▼

35 Mark the centre line on the seat cross rail. ▼

36 Take the two centre back slats, and place them in their fanned position on the seat cross rail. When you are happy with this position, mark it in pencil and hold the slats in place with two G-cramps. ▼

37 Now mark each tenon shoulder line at the top of the slat with a marking knife. Remove each slat from the frame, pare the tenon shoulder accurately to the cut line. The two slats can now be pushed home into the tenons.

38 The bottoms of the slats are waisted where they are screwed to the seat cross rail. This is to allow the seat slats to fit between them. Mark the waisting on the two centre back slats. Take the seat slat that will fit between them, and mark the waisting on it as well. ▼

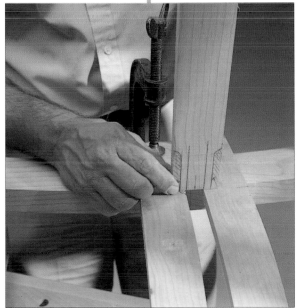

39 To get the curved edge on the waisting, start with a drilled hole, then saw, and finish the curve with a spokeshave. ▼

FURTHER INFORMATION	
24-25	Planing
44-46	Making a mortise and tenon joint
70	Holding and cramping
164-165	Shaping wood

41 Continue fitting the rest of the back slats: mark the position on the seat cross rail, mark and cut the tenon shoulders. Fit the tenons, waist the ends of the slats, drill screw slots, and screw in place. Notice the mortise and tenons are not yet glued.

40 Drill screw holes. If you cut slots for the screws instead of holes, they will allow for any slight movement when sitting in the chair, and will relieve the top tenons of any stress. ▼

FIT SEAT SLATS

42 Starting with the centre slat, waist the slat where it will be screwed to the seat cross rail. Waist the other slats and place in the fan position. Mark the recesses for them on the front rail. ▶

43 Remove the rail again from the frame and cut the recesses. This can be done either by hand with saw and chisels, or with a router.

44 Replace the front rail in the frame and finally fit the seat slats. You will find that due to the curvature of the seat and front rails the rear of the slats will not sit flat. Work the angle to enable each slat to fit. Drill the hole and fit the screw. ▶

45 Mark the length of the slat and trim if necessary to ensure that it seats snugly in the recess on the front rail. Drill the front hole and screw into place. Repeat with the other slats. ▶

FINAL ASSEMBLY

46 Remove all screws, slats etc. and sand down all components (but do not remove your identification numbering).

47 Assemble the main seat frame, apply glue to the joints on the three cross rails and cramp up the frame. Remember to check for square and remove surplus glue. ▶

48 When the glue has cured, remove cramps and finally sand. Finish the frame, but mask the mortises on the top back rail.

49 Mask the tenons on the top of the back slats and sand and finish all the slats.

50 Fit the back slats, applying glue and light cramping procure to pull the mortises and tenons together. Screw the slats at the bottom, then remove cramps. Then screw the seat slats into place.

51 Finally, check the finish. Apply a coat of wax polish if required.

52 The finished easy chair, elegant and comfortable. ▼

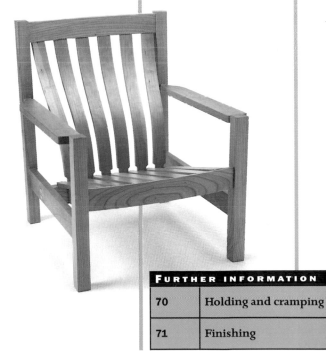

Shaping Wood

Much woodworking is based on the square or linear approach used in cabinetmaking. Making curves and free shapes in solid timber call for different techniques and can be a very satisfying aspect of woodwork.

The techniques introduced here are often used in chairmaking, and as an example, they are shown being used to produce a cabriole leg, a style found in antique and replica chairs and tables. The same techniques are also used in much freer shaping for wood carving and sculpture.

Detailed drawings are essential. For more complicated shapes, make a rough model or prototype from some easily shaped material like balsa wood, polystyrene or plaster of Paris so that you can see the form from all angles and be sure you are achieving the shape you want.

CUTTING CURVES

Curves are imposed on wood grain and do not always follow it. Where a curve results in "short grain" the wood will be weaker and more liable to break than where the length of the grain is used. Always bear this in mind when planning a project. You may need to attach an extra piece of wood with glue, screws or dowels to overcome the problem. ▲

SAWING COMPLEX COMPONENTS

1 The cabriole leg is complex in shape, especially when seen in three dimensions. Initial drawing and planning are the all-important first steps. Draw the shape out on one face, then on the second and on the ends. ▲

2 A bandsaw is the best tool to use to make the first cuts. A power jigsaw, coping saw or bowsaw can also be used. ▼

3 The main object of this sequence of cuts is to ensure that the timber remains a square block for as long as possible so that as much waste removal as possible can be done safely with bandsaw or jigsaw cuts. ▼

4 Cut the few remaining webs by hand with a coping saw. This removes the bulk of the waste. ▶

5 Begin the initial convex shaping with a spokeshave. Cut with the grain on a push stroke and rotate the work in the vice to ensure you are always cutting more or less horizontally and with the grain. Where outside curves are too tight for a spokeshave, use a chisel. ▶

6 Use a convex-soled spokeshave to smooth inner, concave curves. Ensure the cut is always with the grain. Where curves are too tight for the spokeshave, use a gouge. ▶

7 For even finer shaping use rasps, the woodworker's equivalent of files. Rifflers are small double-ended rasps. Their intricately curved ends mean they can smooth wood in awkward corners where no other tool can reach. ▼

8 To summarize, work down through different kinds of abrading and shaping tools, from saws to spokeshaves, gouges and rasps until you have a smooth enough finish to move on to sandpaper, working down through the grades. Make different profile sanding blocks from dowel or piping, and battens and pieces of scrap wood to suit the shape of the work. ▼

OTHER SHAPING TOOLS

A Surform file is coarse and removes material quickly. It is often too coarse for woodwork, but can be very useful for shaping models or mockups made from materials other than wood. ▲

The drawknife is a very ancient woodworking tool used for fast shaping of components before they are more finely finished by a spokeshave. The blade is bevelled on one side and the tool cuts on a pull stroke in the direction of the grain. Hold the drawknife bevel upwards to work a convex shape; hold bevel downwards for a concave shape. ▲

The finger file is a narrow-belt power sander. It removes wood very fast and is best for the earlier stages of shaping. ▼

A flexible drive attached to a power drill can hold a range of small rotary rasps and burrs. These can reach into very close curves.

FURTHER INFORMATION	
9	Safety first
50-53	Advanced hand tools
76-77	Power hand tools
92-93	Machine tools

Bending and Laminating

It is not always possible to produce shaped components by cutting shapes from solid timber because short grain can make a component prone to failure.

Bending and laminating in a home workshop are generally confined to making a shape in one plane. It is possible to make steam bends in several planes, and it is possible to make panels with double curvature, but this needs quite advanced industrial machinery.

There are, however, several ways to create simple one-plane shapes.

BRICK OR STACK LAMINATING

This is a traditional method often seen in serpentine-shaped rails or bowed drawer fronts. The curved stack once completed is often veneered.

The method is rather like building a brick wall with shaped blocks of wood which are then glued together. It is essential to make a full-size drawing of the shape you want to form. From this you

can decide on the best positioning of the brick courses to achieve a strong structure. ▲

1 Make a cardboard pattern for the bricks. Build the shape, adding one layer at a time and allowing the glue to cure between layers. ▲

2 Smooth the surface with planes and spokeshaves when the required height has been reached. ▶

SAW KERFING

This is a method of bending a flat sheet of either solid wood or manmade board. The principle is based on the removal of a series of saw cuts or kerfs to a depth through the wood where the remaining material is capable of bending. Bending the material brings the tips of the saw kerfs together. ▲

1 This method needs very careful calculation and a full-size drawing. You must ensure that you know the precise width of the saw kerf and calculate the distance between kerfs to give the required bend. ▲

2 To calculate the spacing of the kerfs, mark the point at which the bending will start and saw a kerf here, leaving at least 3mm (1/8in). Measure and mark the radius of the curve from this first kerf. ▲

3 Clamp one end of the wood firmly, then lift the free end until the kerf closes. Wedge the free end in position at this point, and measure the distance between the bench and the underside of the board. This is the distance between kerfs. ▲

4 Sawing the kerfs with a radial arm saw is accurate but creates a fairly wide kerf unless you use a thin blade. Mark the distance between kerfs in pencil on the guide fence. ▶

5 Other methods of sawing kerfs require a batten clamped to the work as a guide. Hand sawing is very labour intensive. A power circular saw requires a thin blade if you are not to cut wide kerfs. ▶

6 You will need formers around which to make the bend. By its very nature this method is not very strong since only the tips of the kerfs are glued. The cavities between them need a gap-filling glue or filler. The bend can be strengthened by applying thin ply to the kerfed face. ▶

BENDING SOLID TIMBER

This traditional technique was used by the woodworkers, called "bodgers" who made Windsor chairs in the beech forests around High Wycombe.

The basic principle is that wood bends more easily when it is wet, i.e. before being seasoned, so if it is steamed it becomes supple once again.

The technique is possible in the home workshop but it needs a lot of work in the preparation of steaming equipment and bending jigs.

Steaming wood involves a lot of trial and error, it is more of an art than a science. Look on it as a way of learning and experimenting rather than just bending wood.

1 Make a simple steaming chamber from a large pipe or tube, which may be of plastic, metal or ceramic, and which can be insulated on the outside. Make bungs to fit both ends. Drill one bung to accept a rubber pipe from the steam generator. Drill the other bung to allow condensed water to escape; the tube therefore needs to be at a slight angle. ▲

2 Find a suitable steam generator, for instance a large metal drum or a pressure cooker and solder a fitting so that the rubber pipe can be attached. Place the steam generator on a heat source. ▲

3 Stack the timber to be bent in the tube, separating it with spacers to allow the steam to pass completely around it. The timber needs one hour of steaming for each 25mm (inch) of thickness. ▶

5 The outside former is composed of a flexible metal strap with handles. Fit the wooden handles and hardwood end stops using bolts. Make the distance between the end stops the same as the length of the wood being bent. ▶

Outside bending former

Inside bending former

6 When the timber has been steamed, act quickly. You may need thick gloves to prevent scalding. Place the steamed component in the metal strap and bend it around the inside former. ▶

4 Inside and outside bending formers are needed. Make the inside former of chipboard or MDF. It must be strong enough to withstand the cramping pressure while the wood dries, and it must offer some places where cramps can be located within the curve. ▲

7 Cramp and then leave the wood for several days to dry out. If you wish to remove and re-use the mould, you can do so after a day and leave the piece to dry naturally, as long as you make a tie across the two free ends to stop the bend springing back. ▶

LAMINATING

Timber cut into thin strips is glued and pressed into shape between male and female formers.

Special thick veneers called constructional veneers usually made from beech are often used for the laminate. The grain follows a longitudinal direction in all the pieces, rather than being set at alternate right angles like plywood.

You can make your own veneers from solid timber, but this method is quite wasteful since the thickness of the saw means you waste as much as you use. Be very careful in following all safety procedures if you do cut your own strips. You will also need a thicknesser planer to thickness the laminate strips.

Laminating is not difficult but it is essential to draw the full-size shape accurately and when producing laminates with several curves, careful planning for cramping procedures is necessary as formers must sometimes be made in more than two parts to accommodate the curves.

1 Make formers from manmade board such as chipboard or MDF. Mark out the shape carefully, allowing for the thickness of the laminates. Ensure the shapes are precise and finish the internal faces of the formers exactly. ▲

2 Make the mould and the laminates wider than the laminated component to allow for cleaning up. Cut the laminates along the grain using a knife and straight edge. A decorative facing veneer may also be included in the laminate. ▲

3 Always make a trial run, bending and cramping the laminates without glue, to check the position of cramps and ensure that everything comes together tightly. ▼

4 Use synthetic adhesive, preferably UF. Wrap the laminates in polythene to prevent the package sticking to the formers. Place it in the formers, tighten the cramps, working from the centre outwards, and leave to cure. To finish trim the face edge, gauge and plane to width. ▼

FREE-FORM LAMINATING

The principle is similar to laminating, but no mould is used.

Bend the shape you want using only a single piece of laminate to begin with. Construct a series of cramping posts to hold the required shape.

When you are sure you can cramp in the required position, mark the position of the laminate in pencil on the posts.

Make up the pack of glued laminates (strips of rubber bicycle inner tube are useful to bind the pack) and then cramp the laminates in position on the support posts. ▼

PRE-FORMING

Instead of laminating strips, pre-forming involves laminating sheets. Sometimes some of the veneer layers may be turned at 90 degrees to the main direction of grain, like plywood, to give more strength across the pre-form.

This method is mainly used in mass production. It is possible to undertake in the home workshop, but it is only really worthwhile making all the necessary jigs if several identical components are needed.

Easy Chair

The ergonomics of an easy chair, the way it relates to the human body, are more complex than for an upright chair. The complexity involved in designing a successful easy chair provides a real challenge, and a wide variety of approaches have been adopted by furniture designers.

The development of chair design in the 20th century vividly demonstrates a relationship between progress in other areas, such as architecture, as well as furniture design. Some of this development is due to the development of new materials, including metals and plastics as well as techniques such as pre-form and laminating.

Even using natural timber and traditional techniques, the possibilities seem endless. While some chairs seem appropriate just for a time and soon look dated, others have become classic.

PRINCIPLES OF SEATING FOR RELAXATION

The back can be at almost any angle from almost upright to almost prone. Remember that, for comfort, the head needs support, so if the back slopes too far it must be extended to support the head, otherwise neck muscles begin to ache.

The height of the seat at the front can fall within a wide range from low to high. Remember a low seat is more difficult for elderly and infirm people to get out of.

If you are designing a lounger, which supports the lower legs and feet, remember you still have to get in and out.

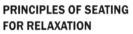
Most support needed
Less support needed
↑ No pressure at these points

ALVAR AALTO • *Paimio chair*
Still a chair that looks very much of today, it is the result of the convergence of a great designer and technological development. Much of Aalto's furniture features the use of laminated and preformed shapes. This is one of the first chairs to use the natural flex of the preformed seat and back to give comfort without the use of soft upholstery. ▲

Relationship between seat rake and depth
If a seat is flat, it needs to be deep and soft to prevent the person from slipping out. ▶

A seat with a deep rake can be short, since the body is held in position and needs the minimum of soft upholstery for support. ▶

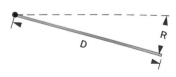

The softness of the seat cushions create a rake as they are deformed by body weight. ▶

An approximate formula for seat rake to depth would be:
Where R=0 (level),
D=610mm (24in)
Where R=130mm (5in),
D=510mm (20in) ▶

JUDITH AMES • *Reflection rocker*
A recent piece, but a timeless variation on the theme of rocking chairs. The colour of the timber and the shaping of all the structural members give great elegance, complemented and enhanced by the back rails and the curve and length of the rockers. ▼

MARCEL BREUER • *Isokon long chair*
Breuer produced many innovative designs, first as a student than as a member of staff at the Bauhaus Design School in Germany during the 1920s and 1930s. When forced to leave Germany he first went to Britain and produced memorable designs, including this one for a laminated *chaise-longue*, before settling in America. ◄

CHARLES EAMES • *670 Lounge chair and ottoman*
This chair is truly a classic piece of design; it is so much of its age, but sits well in interiors of all ages and styles. The combination of aluminium supports, rosewood veneered preforms, black leather and down fillings, combine to give great comfort as well as supreme elegance. One of the masterpieces of 20th century chair design. ►

Chair sizes
The optimum measurements given here are suitable for adults of average height and build. ►

h=250mm to 400mm (10in to 16in)
ht = 394-432mm (15½-17in)
d=610mm to 510mm (24in to 20in)
r=0 to 150mm (6in)
Col (Centre of lumbar) =200mm (8in)
sh=510mm (20in)
n=560mm (22in)
h=200m (8in)

ad=300mm (12in)
ah=100mm (4in)
ar=0 to 50mm (2in)
l=560mm (22in)

w=460mm to 610mm (18in to 24in)
wba=510mm (20in) minimum

Index

Credits

Quarto would like to thank all the furniture makers who have kindly allowed us to include their work in this book.

We would also like to thank the following for their permission to reproduce copyright material: p. 31 *Good Woodworking* magazine; p. 90 & 91 (Robert Venturi) Knoll International; p. 120 & 121 (Hans Wegner) PP Mobler APS, Denmark; p. 151 (Andrew Whateley) photo by Frank Thurston; p. 170 (Alvar Aalto) Artek, Helsinki; p. 171 (Charles Eames) manufactured by Vitra Ltd, London; (Marcel Breuer) manufactured by Windmill Furniture, London.

In addition, Quarto would like to give a special thanks to Axminster Power Tool Centre, Chard Street, Axminster, Devon, who very kindly lent the tools and equipment featured in this book.

AUTHOR'S ACKNOWLEDGEMENTS

In writing this book I am aware of specific thanks needed, but also a sense of general support from the many woodworkers I have known. Specifically, thanks to my wife Raye and to Quarto's staff for their help and encouragement. Generally, however, having been concerned with the woodworking and furniture trade for over 30 years, and also been involved in craft and design education, I remember my many colleagues and friends. The world of furniture craftsmen is full of interesting and lively people who gain pleasure from designing and making fine pieces that in themselves give pleasure to the recipients. I recognize and thank them for their influences. I have taught in many education institutions and I must thank my many colleagues for their interest and support. I have been fortunate to have known many students in furniture making and design studies, and have gained much enjoyment from seeing them develop and then utilize their skills, especially those from Rycotewood College and the School of Architecture at Oxford Brookes University. In particular, I would like to thank the staff and students of the Furniture College at Letterfrack, Co. Galway, in the Connemara area of Ireland, and especially graduate Joel Friel who helped make the prototypes.